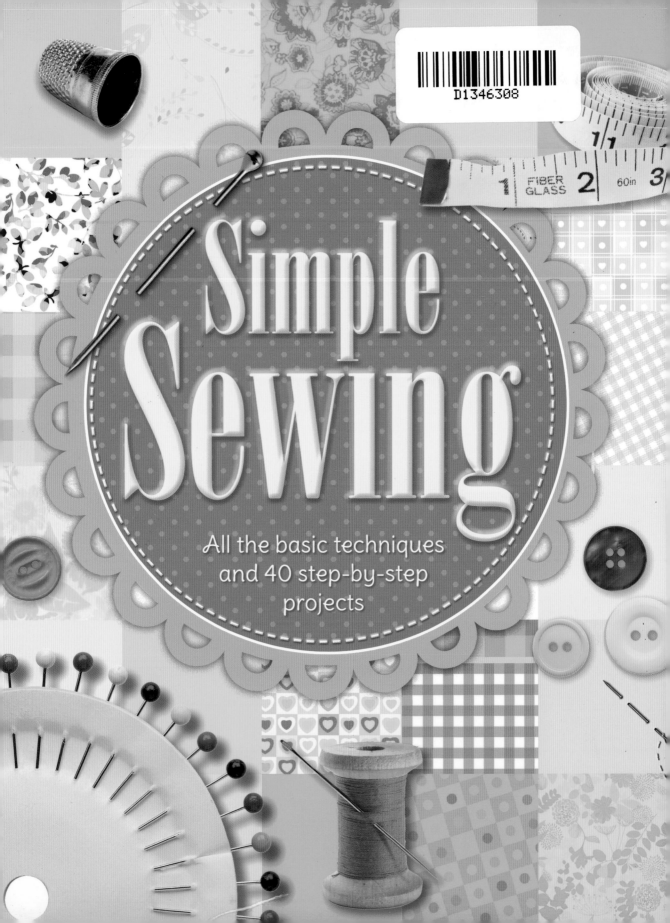

Simple Sewing

All the basic techniques
and 40 step-by-step
projects

D1346308

Simple Sewing

All the basic techniques and 40 step-by-step projects

igloobooks

igloobooks

Published in 2013
by Igloo Books Ltd
Cottage Farm
Sywell
NN6 0BJ
www.igloobooks.com

Copyright © 2013 Igloo Books Ltd

All projects, content and images supplied by Sew Hip

All rights reserved. No part of this publication may be
reproduced or transmitted in any form or by any means,
electronic, or mechanical, including photocopying, recording,
or by any information storage and retrieval system,
without permission in writing from the publisher.
The measurements used are approximate.

FIR003 0213
2 4 6 8 10 9 7 5 3 1
ISBN 978-1-787197-316-5

Printed and manufactured in China

a guide to
Sewing

igloobooks

Contents

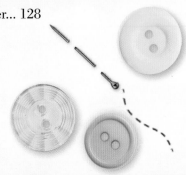

Introduction

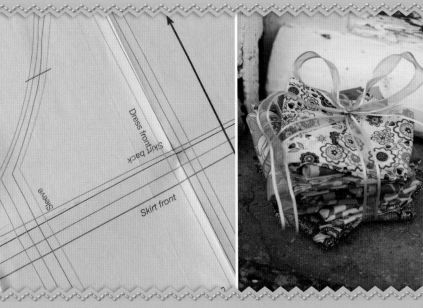

Follow the step-by-step sewing instructions
in this comprehensive how-to guide and
learn to create your own stylish garments,
fun accessories and charming homewares.

A GUIDE TO SEWING MACHINE
Needles

All you ever wanted to know about sewing machine needles but were afraid to ask!

A common mistake often made by beginners is to use the same needle for everything you sew. The size of the needle that you need for a specific job depends on the size of the fabric yarns in the fabric you are sewing. For example, if you are sewing a fine fabric then you need to use a fine needle, which needs to be fine enough not to mark the fabric and yet still have a big enough eye to ensure that the thread does not break or fray while you are sewing with it.

With so many different needles out there, all with seemingly bewildering names, how do you know which one to choose?

Sharp points (regular)

For use with woven fabrics because they cause a minimum amount of puckering and produce an even stitch without damaging the fabric. It is not recommended for use with knits because it can cause skipped stitches.

Sharp points are more slender through the shaft and should be used when edge stitching on woven fabrics, sewing on finely woven fabrics or heirloom stitching

very fine fabrics. They are also a good choice when sewing with synthetic suede. These needles come in varying sizes from the finest size 9 to the heaviest size 18.

Ball-point needles

Specifically designed to be used with knitted and stretchy fabrics. Ball-point needles have a rounded point rather than a sharp one so they push between the fabric yarns rather than piercing them the way the sharp points do. This eliminates any potential damage to knitted fabrics.

These needles should be used when sewing with interlock knits, coarse knits and other fabrics that will run if snagged. The needles come in varying sizes from 9 to 16. The larger the size of the needle, the more rounded the needle point is.

Wedge-point needles

Designed for use with leather and vinyl, these needles will easily pierce these fabrics and create a hole that will close back up on itself. The wedge shape makes

it a superior needle for piercing tough, unyielding fabrics, such as leather or suede. However, if you're sewing synthetic leathers or suede, it's better to use a standard needle because a wedge point needle will leave a large hole and weaken the seam.

These needles come in varying sizes from 11 to 18. The smaller sizes are suitable for softer, more pliable leather, while the larger sizes are designed for sewing heavy leathers, or multiple layers.

Embroidery needles

These have a larger eye to accommodate the thicker embroidery threads. They also have a special scarf (the groove above the eye) that protects decorative threads from breaking.

"The size of the needle that you need for a specific job depends on the size of the fabric yarns in the fabric you are sewing."

Quilting needles

Also called Betweens, these have a tapered point that allows you to stitch through more layers of fabric (usually the quilt sandwich) and across intersecting seams. The tapered point prevents damage to pricey, heirloom-quality fabrics. They are usually smaller and stronger than regular needles with a small eye, and come in sizes 9 (largest) to 12.

Universal-Point needles

Have a slightly rounded point, similar to the ball-point needle, and are used for general, everyday sewing of woven or knitted fabrics. The needle is tapered so it slips through the fabric weave of the knit easily while still retaining enough sharpness to pierce the cloth. They come in many different sizes with 14/90 and 11/75 being the most popular.

Size of Needle

Once you know which is the right type of needle to use for a sewing project, it's also important to know which size of needle to use. Although there are exceptions, as a general rule, the needle size is judged by the type of fabric being sewn.

MEDIUM-WEIGHT FABRICS

If sewing with slightly heavier weight fabrics such as gingham, poplin, linen, muslin, chambray, wool crepe, flannel, knits, jersey, wool, wool suiting or stretch fabrics, a size 14 needle is generally best.

LIGHTWEIGHT FABRICS

When using lighter weight fabrics such as synthetic sheers, batiste, taffeta or velvet, a size 11 needle would be the normal choice.

MEDIUM-HEAVY FABRICS

Sewing with fabrics such as gabardine, heavy suiting or tweed would require a size 16 needle.

HEAVY FABRICS

When using heavy-weight fabrics such as denim, ticking, upholstery or canvas, a size 18 needle is the most suitable.

DELICATE FABRICS

When sewing with extremely delicate fabrics such as silk, chiffon, voile, fine lace or organza, a fine size 9 needle would usually be the best choice.

Main image:
Invest in a variety of needles that are easy to keep organised – many packs also offer advice on which needle is best for which fabric.

"Always replace a dull or damaged needle straight away. Damaged needles can cause skipped stitches and tearing of your fabric."

A GUIDE TO
Fabric Types

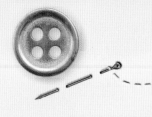

Do you know your burlap from your chintz, or moleskin from ticking? Here's our brief guide to the most common fabrics.

Brocade

A dense weave with the appearance of all-over embroidery. The silk version is most often used for formal wear, while you'll find the cotton version for upholstery.

Burlap/Hessian

Often woven from hemp, jute or raw cotton, it's best used for curtains, wall hangings and sacks. It's also a great base for embroidery.

Calico

A light cotton fabric used for children's clothes and home furnishings.

Candlewick

Famous for bedspreads, this tufted fabric is thick and soft.

Canvas

A heavy fabric that's most often made from cotton, but is sometimes made of a blend of natural and synthetic materials.

Cheesecloth

A lovely lightweight, loosely woven cotton fabric. Used for summer-weight tops and dresses, although as the name suggests, it was originally used in the production of cheese.

Chiffon

Made from silk or polyester, this formal wear fabric is light with a good drape. It works well for multi-layered garments, and for those with tucks and gathers. Use a fine needle to construct the seams.

Chintz

This most often floral-printed fabric is used for heavyweight curtains and upholstery. Synonymous with the English country cottage look.

Cotton

Comes from the seed pod of the cotton plant. It forms the basis for a plethora of fabrics, on its own in muslins and canvas, or spun with polyester.

Corduroy

A fabric with a rib effect, usually cut with the stripes falling vertically. Available in different weights – the heavier the weight, the wider the ribs.

Crêpe

Woven with a twist in the fibres, this fabric has an almost creased look to it. Sometimes it is backed with satin.

Crêpe de Chine

Mostly made from synthetic fibres rather than the traditional silk, this lightweight, plain-weave fabric is used for evening wear and blouses.

Damask

A firm weave of cotton, linen or blends, often forming a pattern with metallic or reflective areas. Often used for interiors, particularly table linen and bedding.

Denim

Famously strong fabric originally used for work clothes, now worn by everyone, whether for work or pleasure. Made with coloured warp and white weft. Use a denim-specific needle with a heavy cotton thread.

Drill

Similar to Denim, this strong weave is made from cotton. There is usually a strong bias (diagonal) in the weave.

Felt

A wool fabric made by agitation and rubbing of the wet fibres; the application of heat fixes it. A great fabric for children learning to sew.

Flannel

Soft, pliable fabric made from wool or cotton blends. Always pre-wash flannel before working with it because it can shrink, but it can also stretch when worn. It's a good idea to add a little to the seam allowance because it has a tendency to fray.

Gabardine

A heavyweight woven twill that's the main fabric for raincoats and sportswear.

Gingham

Cute cotton fabric, woven to give an almost chequerboard effect. Used for cottage-style interiors and children's clothes.

Jacquard

"Always pre-wash flannel before working with it because it can shrink, but it can also stretch when worn."

Named after its inventor, Joseph Jacquard, this heavy fabric is woven on looms, with a raised surface and often with images. You'll find this fabric adorning upholstery in many stately homes.

Jersey

A common name given to 'knitted' versatile fabrics. Has a tendency to stretch width wise. It's best to hem jersey with a twin needle to top stitch.

Lamé

This name is given to fabrics that are woven with metallic fibres.

Linen

The fibres of the stalks of the flax plant are used to make this fabric. It's known for creasing heavily but it's possible to purchase some linens that have been blended with synthetic fibres that crease less. For best results, sew using a cotton thread with 9-12 stitches per inch.

Moleskin

No moles are killed in the making of this heavy fabric. It's actually cotton based, which is then brushed to create a suede-like quality.

Muslin

A cotton weave that comes in various qualities. Dressmakers like to used it to make 'dummy' garments before cutting the actual, intended material to size.

Net

Most often made from nylon, this open, knotted fabric has hexagonal-shaped holes.

Polyester

A product of the petro-chemical industry, this fibre can take on the appearance of silk, blend with other fibres, or be turned into batting for quilts and stuffing for toys.

Satin

Not exactly a fabric type, but the name given to a particular weave of silk, cotton and polyester. Needle and pin marks will show on satin, so check all measurements before sewing. It's also a good idea to change your needle regularly to avoid it snagging.

Shot Silk

This is the effect achieved when the weft and the warp of the weave are different colours. As the fabric moves, it appears to take on a different colour.

Silk

Comes from unwinding the cocoon of the silk worm. It's a strong yet delicate fibre, and has been discovered as being used over 5,000 years ago in China.

Taffeta

Made from cotton, polyester or silk, this fabric has a subtle sheen but it also rustles when it moves.

Ticking

The most common use for this fabric is pillowcases. It's recognisable by its white/cream background with blue stripes.

Tweed

Woven from pure wool, often with slubs of another shade running though it. Its hard-wearing nature makes it the perfect fabric for making suits.

Velvet

A weave with a short-cut fibre, traditionally made from silk fibre, but nowadays also woven from synthetics.

CHOOSING
Thread

There are many different types of sewing thread that should all be used for different projects. Join us in investigating some of the most commonly used ones.

The type of thread that you use when sewing a particular project will be chosen based on the type of fabric you are using, and the project that you are sewing.

There are many different types of thread available to buy, but we are going to look at ones that you are most likely to use with your sewing machine. Thread comes in different thicknesses, general purpose threads tend to be medium thickness of about size 50. Cotton is the most commonly used thread and is available in a huge array of colours. You are most likely to use cotton thread if you are sewing linen, rayon or medium weight cottons.

Most cotton threads are mercerized, which means that the thread is smooth and shiny. It is not advisable to use cotton thread for sewing on jersey projects, as the jersey fabric is very stretchy and cotton has no stretch.

Fine silk threads are most often used for sewing on silk and wool. The make up of this thread gives it quite elastic qualities, meaning that it can be used on jersey fabrics with some success. Silk threads are also idea for basting stitches because it is very fine and so will not leave holes when you remove the stitches at the end of the project.

Alternatives

You also have the choice of using nylon or Polyester threads when sewing light to medium-weight fabrics. Polyester is good for using on stretch fabrics, as well as knitted and woven fabrics. Many polyester sewing threads will be coated with silicone to minimize friction as you are sewing with them, allowing them to freely flow through your machine. Another alternative to cotton/polyester threads is a hybrid of the two. Cotton wrapped polyester gives you the best of both types of thread. It is strong and elastic with a tough, heat-resistant surface.

Cotton, polyester and the cotton wrapped polyester in heavier weights also available and are most suitable for sewing upholstery fabrics or heavier weights of clothing. If you are unsure which thread is best for your fabric, your local haberdasher will be happy to help.

"The type of thread you use in your next sewing project will depend upon the type of fabric that you are going to be sewing."

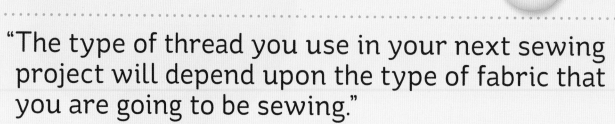

Basic Stitches

There are many different types of sewing thread that should all be used for different projects.
Join us in investigating some of the most commonly used ones.

Chain Stitch If you want to create thick, pretty lines quickly, this is the stitch to use.

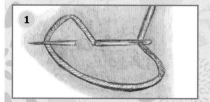 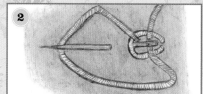 

Step 1

Pull the needle to the right side where you want your chain-stitch line to start. Insert the needle close to where your brought it up and without pulling it through, bring the needle up approx 0.5cm (¼in) along the line, looping the thread under the point. Pull the needle through and tease the stitch to make it even.

Step 2

Now push the needle back through the fabric, very close to where it came up in the loop, and bring it up 0.5cm (¼in) along the line you are following. Loop the thread under the point of the needle again and pull the needle through, again teasing the stitch to even it out.

Step 3

Repeat step two until you have a length of chain stitches. Keep the stitches even by leaving the same 0.5cm (¼in) gap and teasing out each stitch as you go. Don't pull too hard on the thread as the fabric may pucker. To finish, secure the last loop with a little stitch at the top of the curve.

Split Stitch Perfect for making curved lines, flower stems and outline stitches.

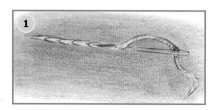 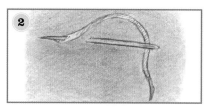

> "Be careful when pressing embroidery with an iron, you could flatten the stitches."

Step 1

It's best to work from left to right. Start by bringing the needle through to the right side, at the point where your line begins. Take the needle down a stitch to the right, then bring it up halfway along the previous stitch, splitting the thread.

Step 2

Place the next stitch to the right of the first, taking the needle back up through the previous stitch as before. Continue in this manner until your line is finished.

Satin Stitch Use rows of close, straight stitches to fill many different shapes for interesting embroideries.

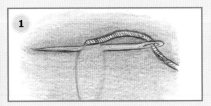

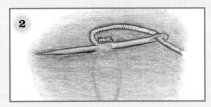

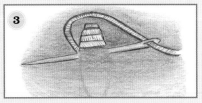

Step 1

If you are unsure about working freehand, use a fading marker pen to mark out your design. Starting at one side, at the top of your shape, bring the thread through to the right side and back down on the opposite edge of your design. Bring the needle up next to where you first brought the thread through.

Step 2

Insert the needle back through to the wrong side, close to where you made the first stitch, then bring it back up through on the opposite side of the shape. Don't pull too tight or the shape will distort.

Step 3

Continue making these parallel stitches, from one side of the shape to the other, until your shape is full. Fasten off the thread at the back of your work.

French Knot Perfect for flower centres, embroidered trees, or interesting patterns.

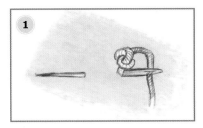

Step 1

Pull the needle through to the right side where you want the knot positioned. Wind the thread twice around the needle and insert the needle very close to where the thread came through to the right side.

Step 2

Holding the stitch with the thumb, pull the needle through to the wrong side and secure the thread, or bring it through to the right side where you want to place another knot.

Satin Stitch Use rows of close, straight stitches to fill many different shapes for interesting embroideries.

Step 1

Lay a line of running stitches along the line that you want to sew and fasten off. Now choose another colour of thread or keep the same thread, and change to a blunt-ended darning needle, depending on the size of your running stitches.

Step 2

Starting at one end of your running stitch line, bring the needle through to the right side, close to the start of the first stitch. Using the blunt end of your needle, weave the thread through your foundation line of stitches, taking care not to pull too tightly.

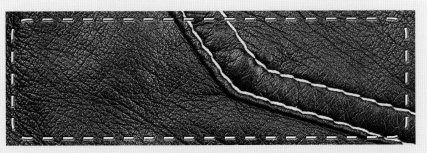

Basic Stitches

Once you have mastered the basic stitches you can add extra detail to garments with more decorative techniques.
Here are a few more stitches to increase your sewing repertoire.

Lazy Dazy
Sometimes called the 'detached chain stitch', you'll most often find it used to make flowers due to the petal shape. Perfect for a quick embellishment.

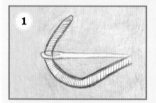  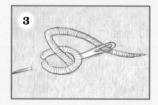 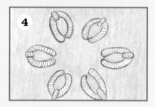

Step 1

Mark on the fabric with a fading marker where you want the stitches placed. Now bring the needle and thread through to the right side at the base of the stitch position. Take the needle down again, very close to this, but don't pull the thread through.

Step 2

Bring the tip of the needle to right side of the fabric to the length that you want your 'petal' to be, making sure the needle point goes over the thread loop and pull through.

Step 3

Take the needle back down to make a small securing stitch and adjust the loop to the shape desired.

Step 4

You can group the stitches together to make a flower formation, or add them to a stem-stitched line to give the look of leaves on a stem.

Bullion Knots
Wind the thread around your needle, to create these effective, large knots.

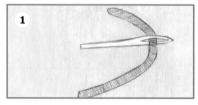 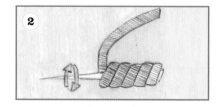 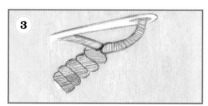

Step 1

Bring the needle up through the fabric where you want to place the stitch and take it back down the same distance that you want the knot to be, but don't pull the thread all the way through.

Step 2

Bring the needle and thread up at the first position and wind the thread from the first stitch around the point by rotating the needle around the thread.

Step 3

Hold the wound thread close to the fabric with the thumb of your other hand and gently pull the needle and thread through. Take the needle down at the other end of the stitch to secure.

Laid Trailing Stitch
Make short stitches over a thread of the same colour to create a 3D feel.

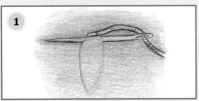 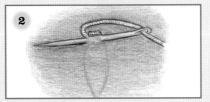 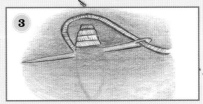

Step 1
Take your needle through to the wrong side of your fabric where you want the line to start, leaving a tail end that is the same length as the line you are creating. Place the loose thread over your work, roughly in the pattern you want to embroider.

Step 2
Bring the needle up, close to the start of the line. Now take the needle down on the other side of the tail thread and pick up a small bit of fabric beneath the loose thread (as if to encompass the thread).

Step 3
The next and all consecutive stitches should be placed close to the previous one. Continue in this manner until the length of the tail thread has been covered.

Long and Short Stitch
Use this technique to fill in large areas of your embroidery.

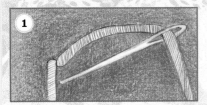 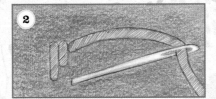 

Step 1
Bring the needle up through the fabric where you want to place the stitch and take it back down the same distance that you want the knot to be, but don't pull the thread all the way through.

Step 2
Bring the needle and thread up at the first position and wind the thread from the first stitch around the point by rotating the needle around the thread.

Step 3
Hold the wound thread close to the fabric with the thumb of your other hand and gently pull the needle and thread through. Take the needle down at the other end of the stitch to secure.

Stem Stitch
By placing short stitches close to each other you can create flowing lines. Great for embroidering swirls, flower stems and other abstract shapes.

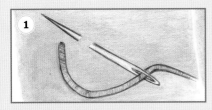 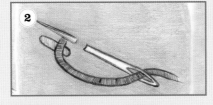 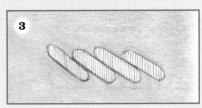

Step 1
It is best work this stitch from left to right. Bring the thread through the fabric where you want the line to start. Then push the needle through to the stitch width, and up again halfway along and to the side the first stitch length.

Step 2
Push the needle through for the next stitch width and bring it up halfway along and to the side of the previous stitch as you did in step 1.

SEWING
TERMS

Our quick reference guide to the sewing terminology that you'll find on the patterns.

Appliqué - Sewing a piece of fabric on top of another for decorative reasons. When done by machine, a satin stitch (tight zigzag) is often used.

Backstitching - Sewing back and forth over the same stitches to lock the end or the beginning of a line of sewing.

Batting - The filling in a quilt. It can be fiberfill, cotton, wool, or other material that is flattened and usually bought by the metre or yard. It is the middle of the quilt sandwich. Also known as wadding.

Bias - Runs diagonally to the straight grain of the fabric. Fabric cut on the bias has more stretch

Basting - The sewing of a temporary stitch. The stitches are large so as to be easily removed. They can be sewn by hand or machine but always with a view to being able to remove them easily.

Binding - Encasing the raw edges of a blanket or quilt with another piece of fabric. Binding can be bought pre-made or made yourself.

Blanket Stitch - A hand or machine stitch that is used to neaten the edge of a blanket, buttonhole or other seam line.

Casing - An envelope of sorts, usually along a waistline or a cuff, which encases elastic or drawstrings, etc.

Darn - To repair a hole by using stitches going back and forth that fill the hole. Some sewing machines come with darning attachments and stitches, which can also be used for free-motion quilting.

Embellish - To add special stitching, appliqués or other decorations to your sewing project.

Facing - Fabric sewn on the raw edge of a garment piece, which is turned under and serves as a finish for the edge as well.

Fat Quarter - A quilting term that refers to the size of a piece of fabric. A fat quarter is ¼ yard of fabric, about 18in x 22in, as opposed to a regular ¼ yard, which is 9in x 45in.

Finish (an edge) - To turn under 0.5cm (¼in) and stitch or serge the edge so that it doesn't fray or have too much bulk.

Fuse - The use of a special material that melts to 'glue' two layers together. The fusing works by being melted with an iron.

Fusible Web - Is available in a variety of weights and sizes.

Gathering - A method of easing a seam to allow insertion of sleeves and other rounded pattern pieces. To gather the seam, two parallel lines are sewn on the right side of the fabric. Long tails of thread are left for gathering. The bobbin threads (on the wrong side of the fabric) are held on either end of the seam and gently tugged, gathering the fabric evenly.

Grain - The direction of the fabric that runs parallel to the selvedge.

Hem - An edge that is turned under to the inside of a sewn item, and sewn.

Interfacing - An unseen addition to various parts of a garment, which adds body that the fabric alone would not add. Interfacing is available in many weights, in woven, knitted and non-woven forms as well as fusible and sew-in forms.

Inseam - The seam on a trouser leg that runs from the crotch to the hem.

Mitre - A technique that gives a corner a smooth, tidy finish, neatly squaring the corners while creating a diagonal seam from the point of the corner to the inside edge. Often used for the corners of a quilt binding.

Notion - A term used for any item used

for sewing other than the fabric and the machine.

Pressing - A different process than ironing. Instead of running the iron across the fabric, you gently lift the iron to press a new area so as not to distort the fabric grain.

Raglan Sleeve - A type of sleeve that extends in one piece fully to the collar, leaving a diagonal seam from armpit to collarbone.

Right Side - The right side of the fabric is the side that the design is on. Sometimes a fabric has no discernible right side, so then it is up to the sewer to decide which is the right side.

Rotary Cutter - A cutting tool used in quilting to cut fabric instead of scissors. Shaped like a pizza cutter, it is perfect for cutting long strips of fabric or many layers at once.

Running Stitch - A simple stitch that is often used for basting or as the basis (marking) for another, more decorative stitch

Serger - A type of sewing machine that stitches the seam, encases the seam with thread, and cuts off excess fabric at the same time. These are used for construction of garments with knit fabrics mostly, or to finish seams of any fabric.

Seam Allowance - The area between the stitching and raw, cut edge of the fabric. The most common seam allowances are ¼in, ½in and 5/8in. Your pattern should say which seam allowance you are to use.

Selvedge - The edges of the fabric that has the manufacturer's information. The information on a selvedge may include colour dots in the order that the colours were printed on to the fabric and lines to indicate the repeat of the pattern printed on the fabric.

Straight stitch - The regular stitch that most sewing machines make.

Top stitch - A sometimes decorative, sometimes functional stitch that is usually ¼in from the edge of a seam.

Tension - There are two types of tension on your sewing machine - the thread and bobbin tensions.

Tack - To sew a few stitches in one spot, by hand or by machine sewing, to secure one item to another.

Wrong Side - The side of the fabric that has no design on it or that you don't want facing outwards. Sometimes there is no discernible wrong side to a fabric.

Zigzag stitch - A stitch that goes one way (zig) and then the other (zag) and provides a nice finish to a seam to prevent fraying, it can also be used as a decorative stitch.

Clothes

Dive into a variety of exciting projects in this fabulous clothing section, and create your very own vibrant, one-of-a-kind garments that you'll love to wear time and time again.

Jersey Dress

Make this simple yet gorgeous jersey dress from one piece of fabric – no cutting is required, just sewing with elastic for an easy-fitting style.

About this Pattern

3 ●●○○○ Difficult

Step
FORM A TUNNEL FOR THE ELASTIC

Distinguish the width of the fabric from the length – the width will be a larger measurement than the length. The length will be 1m (1yd). Along the width, fold the fabric over by 0.5cm (¼in), then fold over again by 1.5cm (⅝in),in the same way as a hem would be made. Stitch this down so that it forms a 1cm (½in) tunnel. Do not add the elastic yet.

Step 2
FIRST SHIRRING LINE

Wind the shirring elastic onto the bobbin, stretching it slightly as you go. Do not overfill the bobbin. Your top thread should match or contrast with your fabric, as it will be visible on the right side of the dress. Set your stitch length (on straight stitch) to at least 4. Test on a scrap of the fabric.

> "Made from a single rectangle of jersey fabric, this dress couldn't be easier to put together!"

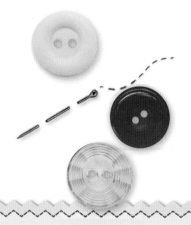

MATERIALS

Double-width jersey – 1m x 1.25m (39in x 49in)

Elastic, 0.5-1cm (¼-½in) wide (see table and pattern notes for details)

Shirring elastic – 1-2 reels

Spare bobbin (for winding elastic)

PATTERN NOTES

We've given suggested elastic requirements in the finished size table, but alternatively, you could measure your chest (above the bust) and take 10cm from the measurements. Pull the elastic around you before you cut – it should not be loose (otherwise the dress will fall down!) but equally, it should not be so tight as to dig into your skin.

It takes a surprising amount of shirring elastic to complete this project, so make sure you have enough. White shirring elastic will be fine for most projects. Choose a matching colour if your fabric is semi-transparent, or choose a contrasting colour and stitch the elastic on the right side of the fabric.

We recommend using a quilter's guide bar when spacing the elastic – it's not essential but will save you a great deal of measuring time!

All seam allowances are 0.5cm, unless otherwise stated.

The fabric will be sewn on the right side. Attach the quilter's guide bar so that it is 2cm (¾in) away from where you will be stitching. Use the stitching of the tunnel as a guide to keeping your next stitch line straight. You will stitch a straight line underneath the line of the elastic tunnel you made previously. Starting from one end (without back-stitching to secure), sew along the length of the fabric. At the end, do not secure the stitching with back-stitches. Start and finish less than 0.5cm (¼in) away from the edges. Note: If you do not have a quilter's guide-bar, mark out the rows with tailor's chalk at an equal distance apart. Follow these with the stitches.

Step 3
NEXT SHIRRING LINE

Once again, line up the quilter's guide bar with the line you just stitched 2cm (¾in) away. As you sew the second line, make sure you pull the previous line of stitching so that the fabric is flat. This will help you to keep the lines straight and keep the gathers even.

If the bobbin elastic runs out mid-row, simply refill the bobbin, then stitch over the last few stitches sewn. These can be tidied up when you tie off the other ends.

Continue in this way until you have made a section that will sufficiently covered the

bust area – measure against yourself to gauge when it's done.

Step 4
NEATEN ENDS

Tie off all the ends individually, then stitch over them in a long line of straight stitch, 0.5cm (¼in) from the edge, on both sides. You will stitch over them again when sewing the side seam.

Step 5
INSERT THICK ELASTIC

Cut your elastic to length. Thread it through the tunnel across the top of the dress – pin one end to the fabric so that you don't lose it within the tunnel. Spread the gathers across the full width of dress. Secure the elastic ends together with a few stitches, then tuck the join in the elastic into one side.

Note: For larger dress sizes, the elastic will be looser than the shirring, but this will be fine because the shirring will stretch as necessary.

Step 6
STITCH THE BACK SEAM

Fold your fabric in half along the length of the dress, with right sides together. Pin the

back seam together. Select a stretch stitch on your machine and sew using a 1cm (½in) seam allowance. Jersey doesn't tend to fray so there is no need to finish the seam, but if you wish, you could finish the seam with a zig-zag stitch.

Step 7
HEM

Since jersey doesn't fray, your fabric may not need to be hemmed. If you do wish to hem the bottom of the dress, simply fold under by 1cm (½in) and press, then fold under by a further 1cm (½in) (to enclose the raw edge) and stitch with a stretch stitch.

Step 8
STRAPS

Straps can be added, if necessary. These could be pre-made bra straps, decorative elastic or fabric-covered elastic.

FINISHED SIZE TABLE

DRESS SIZE	8	10	12	14	16	18	20	UK
BUST	77	82	87	92	97	102	107	cm
WAIST	59	64	69	74	79	84	89	cm
HIP	83	88	93	98	103	108	113	cm
ELASTIC REQUIRED	67	72	77	82	87	92	97	cm

Delilah Skirt

A simple A-line skirt pattern that is fun to make and to wear.

About this Pattern

2 ●●○○○ Intermediate

Step 1
CREATE PATTERN

Measure your waist and add on 4cm (1½in). Divide this number by 2. Your skirt pattern needs to be this amount wide at the top and twice as wide at the bottom. Make the length as long as you want the skirt to be, making sure you allow for the hem and skirt casing.
Cut front and back panels using this template.

Step 2
FINISH EDGES

Zigzag stitch all the raw edges of the pattern pieces to ensure they are neat.

Step 3
INSERT ZIP AND JOIN SEAMS

With right-sides facing, pin down one side seam. Mark 15cm (6in) from the waistband and sew to the hem leaving a 1cm (½in) allowance. Press the seam to the waistband. Pin in place the zip, right-side to the wrong-side, and attach using the zip foot on your sewing machine. Sew the second seam the same way.

SIZE
UK dress sizes, 10, 12, 14, 16

MATERIALS
1.8m (2yd) upholstery fabric
15cm (6in) zip
3.5m (4yd) of 2.5cm (1in) wide velvet ribbon

TEMPLATES
Please see step 1.

Step 4
TURN WAISTBAND

Turn the waistband over 0.5cm (¼in), press with an iron and stitch in place. Attach the velvet ribbon to the outside waistband ensuring that the edges are neat where they meet the zip.

Step 5
BOTTOM HEM

Attach velvet ribbon to bottom hem of skirt using a matching thread ensuring that it is level all the way around.

Sew Simple
Shrug

This light, summery shrug will keep your shoulders and arms covered on chilly evenings.

Step 1
CUT FABRIC
Cut two out of the three fat quarters as per the cutting list.

Step 2
JOIN FAT QUARTERS
Sew the fat quarters together using 0.6cm (¼in) seam allowance, using the photograph right as a guide.

Step 3
NEATEN EDGES
Sew a 0.6 cm (¼in) seam along both long sides of the rectangle.

Step 4
JOIN EDGES
With right-sides facing, fold the rectangle in half widthways, sew for approx 38cm (15in) in from either end or to within 7.5cm (3in) of your shoulder.

Step 5
FINISH
Turn the right side out and try it on. Adjust the arm seams as necessary.

About this Pattern

1 Beginner

MATERIALS

3 fat quarters

FINISHED SIZE

53cm x 1.3m (21in x 52in)

CUTTING LIST

Cut two of the fat quarters in half so that you have four pieces that measure approx 53cm x 23cm (22in x 9in).

PATTERN NOTES

We chose to have the hand ends of the shrug in the same material, but you could make this more patchwork or all-in-one fabric if you prefer.

Layered Skirt

A simple A-line skirt pattern that
is fun to make and to wear.

About this Pattern

3 ●●●●○○ **Difficult**

Step 1
CUT TOP LAYER

Refer to the table below and cut a piece
of fabric measuring, 109 (114, 119, 124,
129, 134) cm, 42 (44, 46, 48, 50, 52) in
long, by 30cm (12in) wide.

Step 2
PREPARE TOP LAYER

Turn the top of the fabric over by 0.5cm
(¼in) and press. Turn over again towards
the inside 2.5cm (1in) and sew in place,
leaving a channel so that you can thread
elastic through for the waistband. Zigzag
stitch the bottom edge of the rectangle and
then sew the ends of the fabric together to
form a tube.

Step 3
MIDDLE LAYER

Cut a piece of fabric measuring, 142 (149,
155, 162, 168, 175) cm, 55 (59, 61, 63,
66, 68) in long, by 35cm (14in) wide.
Again, zigzag stitch the bottom of the
rectangle and also the top before sewing
the ends together like a tube. To make
the simple gathers, sew a zigzag stitch
along the edge to be gathered. Thread
an embroidery needle with thick thread.
Using the needle thread the yarn under
the stitches. Pull the yarn, gathering the
fabric to desired width. Secire well at the
end to keep the gathers from coming out.
Distribute the gathers evenly and then
stitch across the gathers with a 5mm seam
to keep them in place. Remove the thick
thread if you desire.

MATERIALS

Use a lightweight cord fabric. See
below for amounts needed and follow
instructions in the text for cutting.

2cm (¾in) wide elastic for waistband.

Size (UK)	8	10	12	14	16	18	
Actual hip measurement	90	94	99	104	109	114	cm
	35	37	38	40	42	44	in
Material needed	2	2	2	2.5	2.5	2.5	metres
	2½	2½	2½	3	3	3	yards

Step 4
ATTACH MIDDLE LAYER

To attach to the bottom of your first tube, keep the top tier of your skirt, right-side facing out.

Step 5
HEM

Cut a piece of fabric measuring 184 (193, 201, 210, 218, 226) cm, 72½ (76, 80, 83, 86, 89) in long, by 30cm (12in) wide. Again, repeat the zig zag stitch, sewing the ends together like a tube and gathering stitches as in step 3. Attach to the bottom of your second panel using the same method in step 4. Sew a 2.5cm (1in) hem at the bottom of this final third panel.

Step 6
WAISTBAND

Thread elastic through the channel you made at the top of the skirt. Adjust it to fit comfortably, cut the elastic and sew the gap closed.

T-Shirt to
Tie-front Wrap

This restyle is a perfect, simple way to update last year's cropped, oversized t-shirt and jazz it up for this summer.

About this Pattern

1 ●○○○○ Beginner

MATERIALS

Oversized cropped T-shirt
Bias binding - 1m (1yd)
Selection of quirky buttons

Step 1
MARK UP T-SHIRT

Mark the centre point of the front of the T-shirt and draw a straight line from the top to the bottom with a fabric pencil. Cut the T-shirt along this line.

Step 2
ATTACH BINDING

Sew the bias binding to the cut edges, starting from the top. Open out the binding, and pin so that the edge of the binding and top are even. Stitch along the binding fold crease then fold the binding to the wrong-side of the top, encasing the raw edges and hand stitch the underside in place. Alternatively, sandwich the cut edge within the folded binding and pin. Select a wide decorative stitch on the sewing machine and thread to match the binding. Sew over the edges, attaching binding at the front and underside as you go. Leave a length of bias binding hanging at the bottom of the T-shirt for ties.

Step 3
SEW BUTTONS

Sew the buttons on one side of the T-shirt at the top near the bias binding. Then repeat with the other side. The buttons may add a lot of weight to the top of the T-shirt so join the cut gap again by sewing a suitable button of your choice over the top of the overlapped fabric and your refashion is complete!

"This is the perfect way to use up any spare fabric scraps and buttons."

Top Tip

Add a square of fusible interfacing underneath the button area to give more support to the garment top.

Headscarf Top

This restyle is a perfect, simple way to update last year's cropped, oversized t-shirt and jazz it up for this summer.

About this Pattern

1 ●○○○○ Beginner

Step 1
CUT FABRIC

Cut two out of the 3 fat quarters as per the cutting list.

Step 2
JOIN FAT QUARTERS

Sew the fat quarters together using ¼in seam allowance, using the photograph below as a guide. JOIN EDGES

With right-sides facing, fold the rectangle in half widthways, sew for approx 15in in from either end or to within 3in of your shoulder.

FINISHED SIZE

This top will fit a UK size 6 - 12. If you need a larger size you can follow these simple instructions by using larger scarves, or squares of fabric with neatened edges.

MATERIALS

2 silky headscarves, measuring approx 50cm (19¾in) square

Handsewing needle

Matching cotton thread

PATTERN NOTES

Enjoy choosing the headscarves for this project. Matching ones would be nice as would complete contrasts.

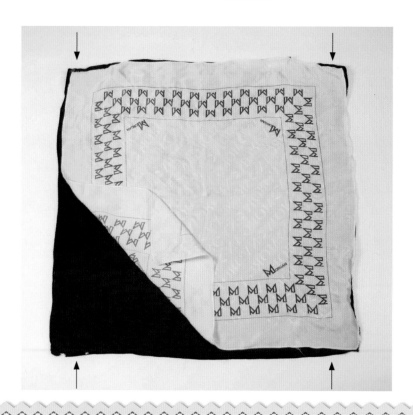

"Use 2 different scarves for a reversible top or the same ones for something simple."

Accessories

This section contains delightful accessories to jazz up your outfits, or they can be given as gifts to your loved ones. Try out new techniques and produce heartfelt, home-made items.

Infinity Scarf

This quick-to-make infinity scarf will see you through spring, summer and winter.

About this Pattern

1 ○○○○○ **Beginner**

FINISHED SIZE

approx 40cm (15¾in) wide by 120cm (47¾in) long.

MATERIALS

Jersey fabric 45.7cm (18in) of 120cm (47¾in) wide fabric

Hand sewing needle

Matching cotton thread

PATTERN NOTES

Jersey is best for this pattern as you don't need to sew the edges, you can leave them to roll naturally and they will not fray. You can use cotton or silk but you will need to sew the long edges and the finished scarf may not drape in the same way.

Step 1
PREPARE FABRIC

Cut your fabric into one length measuring approx 40cm (15¾in) wide by 125cm (49¼in) long.

Step 2
SEW SEAMS

With right-sides facing, sew the two short sides together leaving a 0.5cm (¼in) seam allowance. Turn the right way around and wear!

Picnic Bag

Carry your lunch in style with this insulated sandwich bag, made using fabric designer Rob Ryan's unique patterns.

About this Pattern

1 ●○○○○ Beginner

MATERIALS

0.5m (½yd) laminated cotton or vinyl

0.5m (½yd) coordinating cotton for lining 0.5cm (½yd) thermal batting or felt 5cm (2in) velcro glue
1 button (optional)

NOTIONS

Sewing machine

Sharp sewing needles

Coordinating or invisible thread

CUTTING LIST

2 x 14cm x 25cm (5½in x 9⅞in) rectangles (sides)
2 x 18cm x 25cm (7in x 9⅞in) rectangles (front and back)
2 x 1.5cm x 15cm (⅝in x 6in) (handle)
1 x 18cm x 14cm (7in x 5½in) (base) 1 x 16cm x 10cm (6²/₈in x 3³/₈in), longest edge cut to a curve (flap)
Note: cut all the above once for the exterior, and once for the interior.

All seam allowances are 0.5cm (²/₈in) and are included in measurements given.

If you'd like to use laminated cotton inside and out, you'll need to make your interior pieces a few millimetres smaller to fit. If you intend to put unwrapped food in the lunch bag, choose a laminate that is safe for prolonged food-contact use.

Top Tip
Use clothes pegs instead of pins to avoid damaging your fabric.

Step 1
MAKE THE HANDLE

Place the strips right-side together and sew down one of the long sides. Trim the seam allowance down to a few millimetres. Open right-side out, and fold the remaining long edge in. Top-stitch down both long sides.

Step 2
ATTACH HANDLE

Position the handle on the right-side of the laminated flap piece, along the straight edge. Stitch in place.

Step 3
ATTACH FLAP

Place the flap and back panel right sides together and seam. Finger-press the seam towards the back panel, and top-stitch along it.

Step 4
PIECE TOGETHER BAG

Place the back panel and the bottom right sides together and seam, taking care not to sew into the seam allowance on this step. Finger-press the seam towards the back panel and top-stitch along it. Repeat for the front and sides. You will be left with a cross-shaped piece of fabric.

Step 5
SEAM THE SIDES

Carefully fold the long edges together and seam. Laminated cotton is stubborn stuff

and you may need to be quite firm with it to get crisp corners. If you need to, use scissors to snip into the seam allowance to help you manipulate it.

Step 6
ASSEMBLE LINING

Repeat steps 1–4 for the interior pieces.

Step 7
ADD VELCRO

Peel the backing off the soft velcro strip. Stick onto the interior cotton flap. Sew around it.

Step 8
ASSEMBLE FLAP

Place the exterior and interior right-sides together, and stitch around the flap edge. Turn right-side out.

Step 9
ADD THERMAL BATTING

Smear a bit of glue on one side and, placing the batting 0.5cm (²/₈in) from the top of the laminated cotton pieces, press onto the inside of the picnic bag.

Step 10
FINISH EDGES

Fold over the raw edges of the laminated cotton and the cotton lining at the top of the bag, and press together. Top-stitch around the picnic bag opening, and around the flap.

Step 11
ADD BUTTON

If you like, you can sew a decorative button onto the flap to add a bit of extra pizzazz, as we did here!

Bow Brooch

Pretty bows make great brooches, or you can use them as hair accessories instead.

About this Pattern

1 ⦿○○○○ Beginner

Step 1
PREPARE MAIN FABRIC

Cut two squares out of fabric that are 16cm (6³⁄₈in) wide by 10cm (4in) tall. Take one of these pieces of fabric, fold it in half with wrong sides facing and sew the top seam together.

Step 2
SEW SHORT SIDES

With the seam still facing out, sew the two short sides together. Turn the right-side out and press. Sew the remaining open side of the square together.

Step 3
PINCH AND SEW
Pinch the centre of this piece together and sew in place.

Step 4
SEW LOOP

Cut a square of fabric that measures 4cm (1½in) by 4cm (1½in). Fold the two sides in to meet in the middle and press. Sew this into a loop around the middle of the pressed fabric to cover up the stitches.

Step 5
PREPARE TAILS

Fold the final rectangle of fabric in half as you did for the first piece, and then fold again so that it is narrower than the original piece was. Using a safety pin, push through the back of the loop and arrange the ribbons as required. Adjust until the ribbons are hanging as you would like and then snip the ends on an angle.

Step 6
FINISH

Sew a small piece of felt on the back of the brooch, attach a brooch back and wear.

FINISHED SIZE
Approx 10cm (4in) from edge to edge

MATERIALS
20cm (8in) piece of fabric
Brooch back
Small amount of felt
Hand sewing needle and cotton scissors

PATTERN NOTES
You can sew this by hand or by machine.

TIME TAKEN
Less than half an hour

Front

Back

45

Top Tip

Experiment with different types of fabric. You could use silk for a drapey, more sophisticated bow.

Coin Purse

This cute little padded purse is perfect for pocket money, or precious jewels! It has a useful little tab for clipping inside a larger bag or attaching to a keyring.

About this Pattern

2 ○○○○○ Intermediate

Step 1
CUT FABRIC AND IRON-ON INTERFACING

Cut all of your fabric pieces and interfacing. Press the interfacing onto the reverse side of your outer fabric and onto the strip of lining fabric for the tab following the manufacturer's instructions.

Step 2
MAKING THE TAB

While the iron is still hot, press the strip in half lengthways. Then fold each half in towards the centre line, pressing each flat and being careful not to burn your fingers. Finally, fold in half again, pressing flat to create a 1cm (½in) strip.

Step 3
SEWING THE TAB

Using the same colour cotton as the lining fabric,

sew down each side, equidistant from the edge, to create an attractive and sturdy 1cm (½in) wide tab to thread through your D-ring.

Step 4
ATTACH THE ZIPPER FOOT

Attach your zipper foot to your machine.

Step 5
SEWING IN THE ZIP: PART A

Sandwich the zip between the lining and outer fabric, as shown, with the right side of the zip and the outer fabric facing. Make sure the zip and the fabric are in line and pin if necessary. If you are using a zip that is longer than your fabric, position the fabric towards the end of the zip, keeping the zip-pull closed and at the other end, out of the way.

SEWING IN THE ZIP: PART B

Sew along the zip edge, allowing the raised bump of the zip to be your guide against the protruding section of the

MATERIALS

2 x 10cm (4in) squares of outer fabric, lining fabric, interfacing and wadding.

1 x small zip – see pattern notes

1 x 1cm (½in) D ring or small key ring

1 x 4cm (1½in) wide strip of lining fabric – see pattern notes

1 x 4cm (1½in) wide strip of interfacing (to match above strip)

FINISHED SIZE

Finished purse measures 8cm (3¼in) square

PATTERN NOTES

This simple pattern can be made to any size. With the length of the zip being the only limiting factor, any size zip will do, as long as it is of equal or larger size to your available fabric. You will also need a zipper foot for your sewing machine.

The size of the tab can also vary in length to your own requirements but make it no shorter than 4cm (1½in) in length – for ease of sewing, you can always trim to size later. Make a long strip so that you can clip off tab pieces as and when you make a new purse.

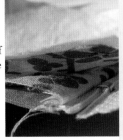

zipper foot. Consider the amount of zip you wish to be showing and set your stitch width accordingly – too close and you risk the zip getting caught.

SEWING IN THE ZIP: PART C

Now you need to repeat the process for the other side of the purse. Flap down the side you have already stitched to reveal the other side of the zip. Make sure you take care to line up the fabric pieces exactly and again pin if necessary. (If you are using a shorter zip, it may be necessary to stop halfway and lift the zipper foot to allow the zipper pull to pass through without causing your line of stitching to be uneven.)

Step 6
SEWING DOWN THE LINING

This is not an essential step but it is important to add quality and stop the lining ever being caught in the zip. When you lay out the fabric, ready to sew the lining down, ensure that you have both of the outer pieces to the other side – you are just adding an extra line of stitching to each lining piece. Pull the fabric pieces gently as you stitch down the line.

Step 7
USE THE ZIPPER FOOT AS A GUIDE
Use the edge of the zipper foot as a guide to ensure that you get an even width along both sides, keeping the stitch width at the same setting.

Step 8
SEWING UP THE EDGES

First, sew up the side of the purse that will not have the tab attached – be sure to position the end cap of the zip inside your line of stitching and be extra careful not to allow your needle to hit the metal cap as you pass from the outer fabric, over the zip and onto the lining fabric. Now sew along the bottom of the outer section of the purse.

Step 9
SEAM WIDTH

Allow a seam width of approx 1cm (½in) in order to leave room for a second line of stitching when you attach the wadding.

Step 10
ATTACHING THE WADDING

Sandwich the outer fabric section of the purse between the two squares of wadding you have cut out. Stitch around three sides to secure the wadding. Use this as an opportunity to add a strengthening second line of stitching all around the purse, leaving the bottom of the lining open to turn through. At this point, trim off any excess fabric.

Step 11
ATTACHING THE TAB

At this point, ensure that your zip is in the open position. Position the tab about 1cm (½in) below the zip with the D-ring facing in. Consider your seam width to judge how far in to position the D-ring. Clip the tab to 4cm (1½in) long and line up the edges with the fabric, giving the tab a seam width of 1cm (½in). Pin into position. As before, sew up the layers, ensuring that the zip is laying flat. Add a few extra lines of stitching to the tab section for strength.

Step 12
TURN THROUGH AND PRESS

Turn through the purse, pushing out all of the corners. Then gently press the raw edges of the lining. Be careful of the wadding, which will melt and stiffen if pressed on a hot iron.

Step 13
STITCH THE LINING

To create a neat finish to the lining piece, press the raw edges in and stitch across. Then push the lining into the purse and that's it – you have a neat little purse!

Pendants & Tags

Play with layering tiny scraps of fabric and trimmings to make miniature appliqués. Turn them into pretty pendants or practical tags.

Step 1
ORGANISE FABRICS

Start with a few fabrics. Sort and cut them into a variety of sizes between 5-6 cm (2in-2¼in) and 1-2cm (½in-⅞in) or even smaller. Layer them in a variety of ways with the small pieces on top of the larger ones. Try not to have more than three layers at any point as it may get too thick to sew.

Step 2
EXPERIMENT

Play with arranging different combinations, experimenting with texture and colour. Try to put things together without agonising over it or giving it too much thought. Just play with the fabric and see what happens.

> "Working small means you can generate a lot of ideas quickly, using small quantities of materials."

Step 3
SEW THE SCRAPS

When several sets of fabric are ready, hold the pieces in place with nimble fingers and stitch the layers together using a narrow to medium width zigzag stitch (Fig. 1).
A variegated thread looks lovely for this. Don't worry if the stitching goes go off the edges, just get back on track and keep sewing until satisfied. Be sure to leave

Fig. I

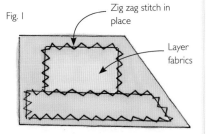

Zig zag stitch in place

Layer fabrics

some frayed edges for decoration.

Step 4
REWORK

Continue to work on more than one appliqué at once. If you don't like a particular sample, try trimming bits off it, cutting it in half and/or joining it to another one, or simply go back and start a fresh one.

FINISHED SIZE
Pendant – 2cm x 3cm (⅞in x 1⅛in)
Key tag – 4cm x 8cm (1½in x 3in)
Bag tag – 6cm x 8cm (2¼in x 3in)

MATERIALS
A variety of recycled scraps of any kind (At least one firm fabric required for the base/backing)
Thread/variegated thread
Beads/tiny buttons
Small eyelets
Thin waxed cord – 85cm (33½in) required per pendant
1 x split ring per tag

CUTTING LIST
All cutting instructions are given within the pattern text.

Step 5
ADD SHAPES OR STRIPS

You can cut small pieces into interesting shapes, leaves, hearts, etc. or stick with squares and rectangles or even go for random abstract shapes. Very thin strips can be interesting too.

Step 6
ADD TRIMMINGS

Add little pieces of lace or ribbon, or other tiny scraps of fabric. Sew on beads or buttons to decorate the tags and pendants (Fig. 2). Try using a decorative machine stitch.

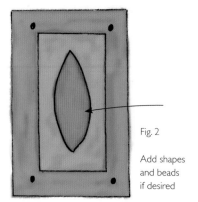

Fig. 2

Add shapes and beads if desired

Step 7
NEATEN APPLIQUÉ

When happy with a sample, trim the appliqué to the final size for the pendant or tag. If you wish to hide the reverse or need additional stability, add a backing layer. Finally, zigzag over the outside edges to neaten them or simply leave them to fray.

Step 8
INSERT EYELET

Following the manufacturer's instructions for the eyelets, insert an eyelet into the pendant or tag.

Step 9
CREATE PENDANT

Fold an 85cm (42½in) length of cord in half, pass the loop through the eyelet from front to back, then pass the cut ends of the cord through the loop and tighten. Adding a few beads to the cord will help to weigh the pendant down so it hangs well. Knot the ends of the cord with an overhand knot to finish.

Step 10
CREATE TAG

Pass a split ring through the eyelet to finish off the tags.

Mug Cosy

Keep your cup of tea warm with your very own funky mug cosy.
A quick 'n' easy sewing project!

About this Pattern

1 ● ○ ○ ○ ○ Beginner

Step 1
MEASURE MUG

To work out the size of your mug cosy, measure the circumference and height of the mug you wish to keep warm.

Step 2
CUT FABRIC

Cut the wadding and backing cotton to the same size as the mug measurements. For clarity, the mug cosy will end up 1.3cm (½in) shorter than the mug's height and 1.3cm (½in) shorter than the mug's circumference. This will allow a large enough gap for the handle.

Step 3
CREATE FRONT

To create the front, cut strips the same height as the mug but of varying widths from the three different types of fabric scraps. Using a 0.6cm (¼in) seam allowance, sew the fabric strips together, long edge to long edge, pressing each seam to one side as you go and alternating the different fabrics.

Keep sewing strips together until you have a rectangle that is slightly longer than the measurements taken from the outside of the mug. Using a rotary cutter and patchwork ruler, neaten edges by trimming to match the measurement taken from the mug in Step 1.

Step 4
BASTE AND EMBELLISH

Using spray baste in a well-ventilated room, spray the wadding and lay the front onto the wadding, right side up. Press front firmly onto wadding, smoothing out any lumps and bumps and let dry before moving on to the next stage.

Now is the time to add any embellishments or stitching to the front of the cosy. We doubled up white thread and hand stitched two large rows of running stitch along the bottom and up the side.

GENERAL NOTES

See Steps 1 and 2 for instructions on cutting.

We recommend washing your fabrics, drying and then pressing them before use so that if they shrink, your project is not compromised.

Seam allowances of 0.6cm (¼in) are included.

MATERIALS

2 x buttons

Thin elastic

Lace

Scraps of three different cotton fabrics

Cotton for backing

Wadding

Contrast thread

Gold thread

Spray baste

TOOLS NEEDED

30.5cm (12in) quilting ruler

Rotary cutter and mat

Pins

Scissors

Measuring tape

Hand sewing needle

Iron and ironing board

Turning tool

Step 5
LAYER FABRICS

Layer fabrics in the following order starting at the bottom: backing right side up, front right side down, wadding. Pin layers together on both long sides and one short side. Between the front and backing on the short side that is not yet pinned, pin two lengths of folded elastic, aligning the cut edges with raw edges of the fabric so the loops are inside the layers (Fig. 1). Pin really well to stop from shifting. We cut ours to 4cm (1.6in) so they would be long enough to reach where we want the buttons on the other side of the cosy. Make sure they don't interfere with where the handles join
the mug.

Step 6
SEW, TURN OUT AND TOPSTITCH

Using a straight stitch, start sewing on the bottom (long) side starting about 5.0cm (2in) away from the corner. When sewing over the elastic, remember to backstitch a few times otherwise the thin elastic may pull free. Carry on around and stop when you have 7.6cm (3in) unstitched along the top edge (Fig. 2). Backstitch to secure. Trim corners to reduce bulk and neaten any edges. Turn the mug cosy right way out and poke the corners out so they are nice and sharp, then press. Press the turning gap so the raw edges are tucked inside and top stitch all the way around a scant 0.3cm (⅛in) from the edge with gold thread, closing up the turning gap as you go. Finally, hand stitch on two buttons on the edge opposite the loops at the same height and your cosy is ready for action!

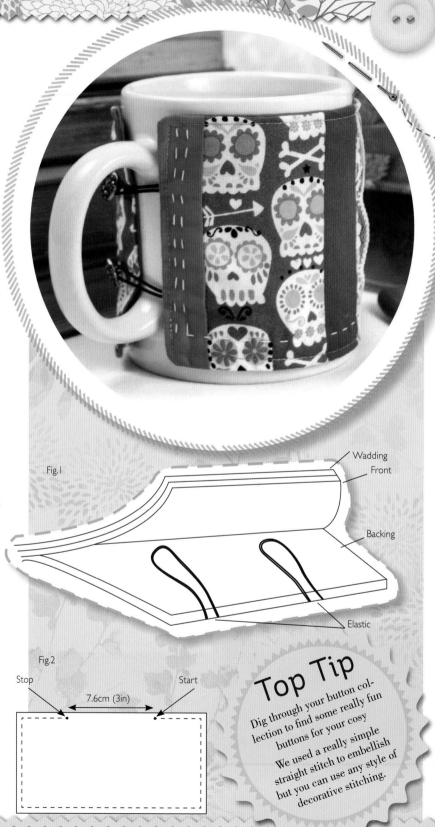

Fig.1

Wadding
Front
Backing
Elastic

Fig.2

Stop
Start
7.6cm (3in)

Top Tip
Dig through your button collection to find some really fun buttons for your cosy
We used a really simple straight stitch to embellish but you can use any style of decorative stitching.

Recycled Scarf

Reuse those summery vest tops and turn them into a jersey scarf to keep you warm in the winter.

MATERIALS

- Adult scarf length 153cm (60in): 3 jersey vest tops, washed and ironed.
- Child scarf length 110cm (43in): 2 jersey vest tops, washed and ironed

PATTERN NOTES

The jersey vest tops should be adult sized, anything from size 8–20 will work.

STEP 1
PREPARE VESTS

Cut across the jersey vest tops 2.5cm (1in) under the armholes. Put the top half to one side and work from the bottom.

STEP 2
CUT SEAMS

Cut up each side seam so that you are left with two pieces of jersey fabric from each vest top. Repeat until you have cut up all sections of the vest.

STEP 3
MAKE STRIPES

You can either leave these pieces the size that they are, or cut them in half width-ways so that you have more stripes.

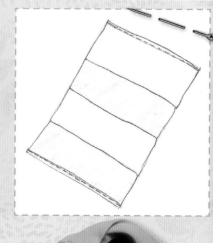

STEP 4
JOIN PIECES

Starting and finishing with a piece of jersey with a hemmed edge, sew the jersey pieces together in a long strip. Decide on a pleasing colour pattern, if you are using more than one colour.

STEP 5
FINISHING

Press seams to one side. Join the long raw edges to form a tube. Neaten seams and turn scarf the right side out.

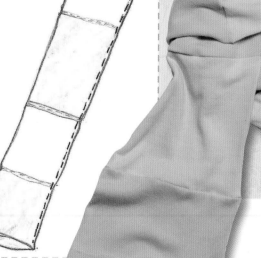

Above:
Mix and match pretty materials for fun and funky scarves.

Rose Wrap

Make your own crinkly, distressed wrap that's a perfect accessory for summer days and nights.

About this Pattern

1 ⬤◯◯◯◯ Beginner

Step 1
FOLD MATERIAL

Fold your material in half lengthways, with right sides facing and sew around the three open sides leaving a small gap. Turn the wrap right way around and sew the gap.

STEP 2
TWIST IT UP

Fold the material widthways so that you have a long, narrow piece of material. Holding one end firmly (you can tie it to a door handle, place it under a heavy weight or ask someone else to hold on to it for you), twist the other end of the fabric around until the twist has gone all the way along the length and it will fold in on itself. Twist it again, if necessary, so that you have a nice, tightly twisted piece.

STEP 3
WET AND DRY

Thoroughly wet the material and hang it out to dry, in the sun if possible. When the twisted fabric is dry, it will be beautiful and crinkly – perfect for wearing as a summery shawl.

MATERIALS
2.7m (3 yds) of lightweight cotton material Matching sewing thread.

Top Tip

The more you twist the fabric, the better! Keep twisting until it wraps round itself and even knot it up. You can also store it this way to keep it crinkly!

Lovely
Bow Clutch

Cute yet practical, this bow clutch bag
is a must-have item for your wardrobe.

About this Pattern

1 ●○○○○ Beginner

FINISHED SIZE
27cm x 15.5cm (10⅝in x 6⅛in)

MATERIALS
115cm (45¼in) printed cotton
115cm (45¼in) lining fabric
115cm (45¼in) stiff non-fusible
interfacing
115cm (45¼in) light weight wadding
27cm (10⅝in) zip
Quilting spray adhesive

CUTTING LIST
From exterior fabric:
1 x main panel 30cm x 33cm
1 x back panel 18cm x 30cm
4 x side bow pieces 29.5cm 17cm
4 x front bow piece 29.5cm 17cm

FROM LINING FABRIC:
1 x main panel

FROM INTERFACING:
1 x main panel

FROM WADDING:
1 x main panel

PATTERN NOTES
All seam allowances are 1cm (³/₈in)
unless otherwise stated.

Step 1
PREPARE FABRIC

Wash, dry, and press the cotton fabric
before cutting. Press the lining fabric on
a low setting. Cut out all pattern pieces
indicated on the cutting list.

Step 2
ATTACH INTERFACING

Match the interfacing with the main panel.
Place the interfacing on the wrong-side of
the fabric. Spray adhesive on the wadding
panel and place sprayed side down onto
the interfacing layer. Smooth the wadding
piece until it adheres to the interfacing

and the edges of the main panel fabric.
Trim off any excess wadding around the
edges. Make sure that the fabric design
is upside down. Fold at the fold lines and
press lightly.

Step 3
BACK PANEL

Press back panel and lay right-side down.
Press the top, bottom and diagonal corners
over by 1cm (³/₈in) to the back (Fig. 1).

Step 4
PREPARE BOW

Take the front bow pieces and measure up
7cm (2¾in) on one of the short sides. Draw
a curved line from this point to the top corner of the other side and cut. Repeat with
other front bow pieces. Take the side bow
piece and fold in half lengthwise. Mark the
centre point on the short edge.

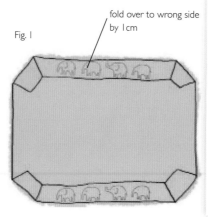

fold over to wrong side
by 1cm

Fig. 1

Measure 3.5cm (1½in) each way from the centre point. Draw a straight line 15cm (6in) towards the other short end. Draw a diagonal line from this point to the corner of the other short side and cut. Repeat with other side bow pieces. Refer to the diagrams below. Place the front bow and side bow with right-sides together, aligning at the centre front edges. Stitch together with a 0.6cm (¼in) seam allowance. Press seam open (Fig. 2). Repeat with the other bow pieces. Take two matching pieces and, placing right sides together, stitch around the edges leaving the sides open. Repeat with all bow pieces. Press open seams, clip curves, and snip corners. Turn right side out and use a blunt pointed tool to make the corners as sharp as possible. You will now have two bow pieces, one left and one right. Press and set aside.

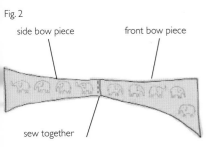

Fig. 2

side bow piece   front bow piece

sew together

Step 5

ATTACH BACK PANEL
Take the back panel and place it on the back of the bag wrong side down. Top-stitch around the edges, leaving the sides open.

Step 6

MAKE LINING

Press the lining at the fold lines. Press open the seam allowance at the zip opening. Pin at the sides, making sure that the shape is retained as per fold lines. Stitch together at the sides with right sides-together.

Step 7

ATTACH ZIP

Take the lower-half edge of the bag and press down seam allowance. Repeat the process with the upper-edge panel. Open the zip and lay it underneath the fold at the top of the bottom panel-edge (Fig. 3). Stitch in place. Repeat process for upper edge.

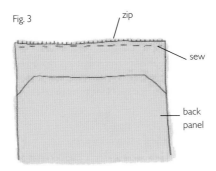

Fig. 3   zip

sew

back panel

Top Tip

For a dressier look, use a plain fabric for the main bag then use a sheer floaty fabric to create the bow on the front.

Step 8

ATTACH BOWS
Turn the bag inside out. Pin bow with raw edges at the side seam. Make sure that the pointed side of the bow end is pointing downwards before sewing. Stitch together unpinning as you go along. Trim edges and clip corners. Turn right-side out. Using a blunt-pointed tool, make the corners of the bag as sharp as possible.

Step 9

INSERT LINING AND FINISH

Place the lining inside of bag. Push corners of lining into corners of the shell. Match pressed edges to the inside-zipper-tape edge and stitch as close as you can to the corners. Hand stitch the lining to the fabric, sewing through all layers at the corners. Lightly press the bag. Tie sashes into a bow and you're done!

Ruffle Belt

This easy-to-make ruffle belt is a great accessory that will liven up any plain T-shirt or dress.

Step 1
PREPARE MAIN PANEL PIECES

Firstly, measure your waist, we will refer to this measurement as "A". This will be the length of the main panel pieces of the belt. Now, cut two strips of fabric from the main belt panel fabric the length of your

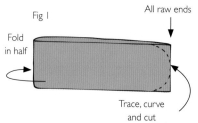

Fig 1

Fold in half

All raw ends

Trace, curve and cut

waist measurement (A) by 9cm (3½in) tall. So if your waist measurement is 70cm (27½in), cut two pieces of fabric 70cm (27½in) by 9cm (3½in).t Round the ends of the main belt panels. To do this lay one panel on top of the other and fold them both in half so all the raw edges of the short ends line up. Round these ends by using a tea cup, saucer, jar or lid to trace a nice curve and cut along the curve through all pieces of fabric (fig 1).

Now use your main belt panel pieces to cut medium weight fusible interfacing of the same, and iron it to the wrong side of the fabric. Press and set aside.

Step 2
MAKE RUFFLE

Multiply your waist measurement times 4. This is the length of your belt ruffle. We will refer to this measurement as "B". Now cut and piece together some fabric to make a fabric strip that is B long by 6cm (2¼in) wide.

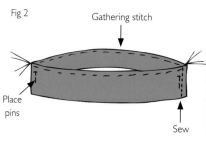

Fig 2

Gathering stitch

Place pins

Sew

FINISHED SIZE

Depends on your custom measurements

MATERIALS

This is a custom made pattern, built to your size, so fabric needs will obviously be different for each person. The following is an estimation:

23cm (9in) to 30cm (12in) for main panels

30cm (12in) to 45cm (17¾in) for ruffle 30 cm (9in) for ties

30cm (9in) medium weight fusible interfacing

30cm (9in) lightweight fusible interfacing

2 pieces of printer paper or one sheet of tissue paper to make pattern

Water soluble fabric peneavy weight interfacing

1 x slider

PATTERN NOTES

This is a custom-made pattern so the fabric needs for your main panels and ruffle will differ as per the size of your belt.

Step 3
ATTACH RUFFLE

Choose one of the main panel pieces to attach the ruffle to (it doesn't matter which one.)

Mark the centre point of each rounded end of the panel. This is where you will place the pins from your ruffle. Match up the pins on your ruffle to the marks on either end of the main belt panel. Be sure that the raw edges are lined up (fig 3).

Now gently gather the ruffle to the main belt panel and pin in place. Make sure the folded edge of the ruffle piece is pointing inwards, and sew around the raw edges to attach the ruffle to the main panel using 0.5cm (¼in) seam allowance.

Step 4
FINISH MAIN PANEL

Place the main panel pieces right-sides together, encasing the ruffle. Sew around the outer edge but leave an approximate 10cm (4in) opening for turning (Fig. 4).

Trim all seam allowances to 0.5cm (¼in) and clip the curves for a neater finish. Turn right-side out. Press and slip-stitch the opening closed.

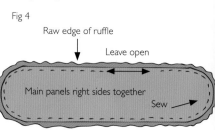

Fig 4

Raw edge of ruffle

Leave open

Main panels right sides together

Sew

Note: If you are working with standard quilting width fabric, you will need to cut multiple pieces from selvage to selvage and sew them together to get a strip long enough. Fold this fabric strip in half, wrong sides together, and press so you now have a strip that is 3cm (1⅛in) wide by B. Sew the ends together to form a loop and mark the half way points on the loop by simply flattening the loop in half and placing pins to mark the folds. Using a 0.5cm (¼in) seam allowance, sew a gathering stitch around the raw edges of the ruffle strip. Start at one pin and stop at the next, then start again at the next pin. This will leave you with threads at the halfway marks and will make gathering easier and more even (Fig. 2).

Step 5
MAKE PATTERN FOR TIES

You will need a piece of paper that is at least 32cm (12½in) long. Draw a 32cm (12½in) long straight line and make points at each end marked A and B. Along this line make dots and label as follows:Make a dot at 2cm (1in) and mark "C"

Make dot at 10cm (4in) and mark "D"

Make dot at 26cm (10¼in) and mark "E" (Fig. 5).

Now centre a 5cm long perpendicular line at points C and D. At point E, draw a 5cm (2in) tall perpendicular line upwards. At point B, draw a 4cm (1½in) long perpendicular line downwards. Your drawing should now look like this (Fig. 6).

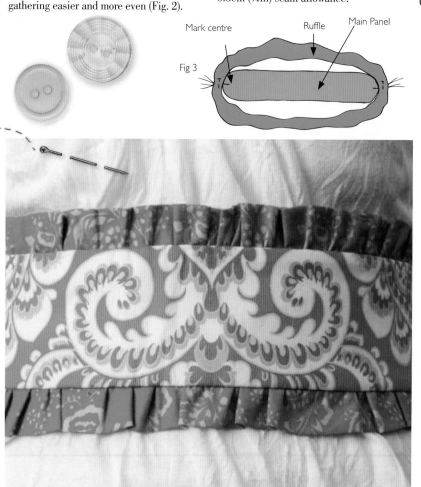

Mark centre

Ruffle

Main Panel

Fig 3

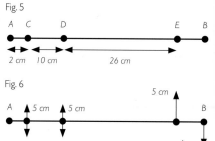

Fig. 5

A   C   D   E   B

2 cm   10 cm   26 cm

Fig. 6

A   5 cm   5 cm   5 cm

B

4 cm

Step 6
CUT PATTERN

Now connect all the lines to form the pattern piece as shown (fig 7). Cut out the pattern piece.

Step 7
SEW TIES

Fold the tie fabric in half with right-sides together. Cut the pattern pieces for two ties. You will be cutting four pieces in total (two at a time as the fabric is folded.)

Take two tie pieces and place them, right sides together, and sew around the edges leaving an opening in the end for turning. Clip all corners and trim seams to 0.5cm (¼in) and turn right-side out. Neatly fold the opening in and press. Top stitch around outer edges. Repeat with the second tie (Fig. 8).

Step 8
ATTACH TIES

Make a placement mark for the tie end on the main panel by measuring 7cm (2¾in) from the center end of the main panel. Place a small dot using a water soluble fabric pen (Fig. 9).

Line up the point of the belt tie with this mark and pin in place (Fig. 10). Sew the tie in place by overstitiching the top stitching on your tie, then sewing a line from the top edge-stitching to the bottom edge stitching. Repeat with the other tie. Your belt is ready to wear!

Fig 7

Join dots and lines

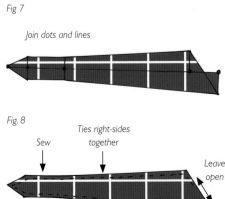

Fig. 8

Sew

Ties right-sides together

Leave open

Fig 9

7 cm (2¾in)

Fig 10

Sew

Pincushion
Sewing Jar

Use up those empty food jars and scraps of material to make these pretty and practical pincushion storage jars.

About this Pattern

2 ●○○○○ Intermediate

FINISHED SIZE
Depending on the size of your jar

MATERIALS
Empty jam jar

Scraps of fabric, approx 10cm (4in) square of fabric for each jar

Ribbon

Buttons

Stuffing

Felt scraps

Fabric / craft glue

Needle and thread

PATTERN NOTES
You can vary the size of the pincushion to match the lid of your jar.

Step 1
DRAW CIRCLE

Draw a circle on the wrong side of your fabric, we used a cereal bowl as our template. You need to ensure that your circle is about twice the size of your lid so if your lid is 10cm (4in) from edge to edge your circle needs to be 20cm (8in).

Step 2
SEW AND GATHER EDGES

With wrong side facing, sew running stitch around the edge of your circle. Gather loosely.

Step 3
STUFF FIRMLY

Fill the circle with stuffing, pull the stitches tight and sew in place.

Step 4
FINISH AND PREPARE BASE

Cut a small circle of felt and glue in place.

Step 5
ADD TRIM

Glue the pincushion top to the lid of the jar and leave to dry. Glue a length of ribbon around the base of the pincushion, fill your jar with buttons or other notions.

Top Tip
Make a whole collection of these jars and use them to store notions and other goodies.

Book Bag

Use up those empty food jars and scraps of material to make these pretty and practical pincushion storage jars.

About this Pattern

2 ●●○○○ Intermediate

FINISHED SIZE
47cm x 36cm (18½in x 141/8)

MATERIALS
Main cotton fabric – 50cm (20in)
Cotton Lining – 50cm (20in)
Firm iron-on interfacing – 50cm (20in)
Packet of small metal eyelets
Zip – 19cm (73/8in)
Bias binding
Narrow cord

CUTTING LIST
From main fabric:
2 x bag body – 49cm x 39cm (19¼in x 153/8in)
1 x top pocket – 10cm x 18cm (4in x 7in)
1 x bottom pocket – 21cm x 18cm (8¼in x 7in)
1 x strap – 9cm x 94cm (3½in x 37in)

From lining fabric:
2 x bag body – 49cm x 39cm (19¼in x 153/8in)

From interfacing:
As main fabric, except: 2 x bottom pocket – 21cm x 18cm (8¼in x 7in)

PATTERN NOTES
Seam allowances are 1cm unless otherwise stated.

Step 1
CUT FABRIC

Cut out all the pieces you will need to make the bag following the instructions on the cutting list.

Step 2
INTERFACING

Apply the iron-on interfacing to the bag body pieces in the main fabric, both pieces of the pocket and the strap.

Step 3
POCKET

Fold both pocket pieces in half with the main fabric to the outside and press. Take the zip and open it right up. Place the smaller pocket piece so that the folded edge lines up with the top teeth of the zip.

Pin in place and stitch along the teeth making sure that the zip stop hangs over the end of the pocket piece (Fig. 1). Take the other pocket piece and place it so that the fold is against the bottom zip teeth and the pocket pieces are level with each other. Stitch along the teeth. Test that the zip opens and closes freely. Trim the zip end so that it is level with the pocket pieces. Pin the bias binding around the entire pocket and stitch into place. Press. Pin the pocket centrally onto the lining so it is 10cm from the top. Topstitch around the pocket on the bias binding (Fig 2).

Fig. 1
sew
folded pocket piece

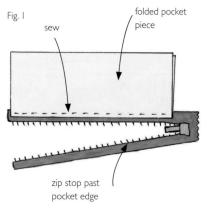

zip stop past pocket edge

Fig. 2 — Lining

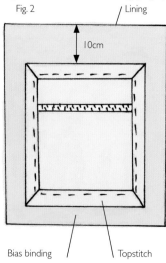

10cm

Bias binding — Topstitch

Step 4
MAIN BAG

Place the main pieces of the bag right sides together and stitch around the sidand bottom.

Top Tip

Why not make the bag in oilcloth for a great swimming bag too?

Step 5
BAG LINING

Place the lining pieces right sides together and stitch as per Step 4 leaving a gap in the bottom for turning.

Step 6
STRAP

Fold both sides of the strap over towards the centre and press. Fold the strap in half and press again. Top stitch down both sides of the strap. Place the strap to the outside of the main bag at the side seams with raw edges matching, and secure in place by stitching across the strap three times.

Step 7
ASSEMBLE BAG

Place the main bag inside the lining with right sides together. Match up the side seams and make sure that the strap is pushed well inside. Pin in place. Stitch around the top of the bag, catching the ends of the strap as you go. Turn out through the gap in the lining. Topstitch the top of the bag and sew the turning gap closed. Press.

Step 8
ATTACH EYELETS

The eyelets need to be placed 10cm (4in) from the top of the bag. Space the eyelets so that on the front there are two central eyelets 6cm (2½in) apart and the other eyelets are 8cm (3in) on either side of these. On the back, place one eyelet close to the left side seam and three eyelets at 13cm (5in) spaces across the back. The tools you need to attach the eyelets are inside the packet with the eyelets. Follow the manufacturer's instructions in the packet (or on the back) for attaching them.

Step 9
FINISH

Thread the narrow cord through the eyelets and secure at the front.

Flower
Head Band

Design your own funky, flowery
headband with this simple, three-step activity.

About this Pattern

1 ○○○○○ Beginner

MATERIALS
1m (1yd) of light weight fabric
Elastic headband

Step 1

CUT FABRIC

Cut six large circles (approx 15cm [5.9in] diameter) and six
small circles (approx 6cm [2.4in] diameter) from a lightweight fabric.

Step 2

CREATE FLOWER

To make the large flower, fold one of the circles
in half with right sides facing. Lay it down on a
clean surface in front of you with the straight
fold vertical. Fold another circle and lay it
on top of the first folded circle with the fold
horizontal, over half of the first folded
circle. Sew in place with a stitch. Repeat
with the other circles layering on top of
the previous folded circles and turning
each one a half turn so that the folds
are horizontal, then vertical.

Step 3

FINISHING TOUCH

Once all circles are sewn together,
pinch underneath and sew in place.
Attach to an elastic headband.

Top Tip
To make the small flower,
repeat with the smaller
circles and attach to
the headband next
to the large one.

Home

Create some wonderful one-of-a-kind pieces for your home that are both useful and beautiful, with this section full of exciting projects. Bring some home-made heart to your living space!

Retro Cushions

Using a plain piece of fabric and a few fat eighths, you can make some beautiful cushions.

About this Pattern

2 ●●○○○ Intermediate

Step 1
CUT STRIPS

For a cushion cover that will fit a 41cm (16in) cushion insert, cut a piece of fabric that is 46cm (18in) tall and 107cm (42in) wide. Measure 30cm (12in) in from each end, fold here and press so that you can see what will be the front of your cushion.

Step 2
MARK CENTRE OF CUSHION

Cut strips of fabric in different widths that are long enough to cover as much of the front of your cushion as you wish to have striped.

Step 3
SEW STRIPS

Sew the strips to the front of your cushion using a zigzag stitch. Overlap them if you wish and arrange them in a pleasing manner.

MATERIALS

5 fat eighths of co-ordinating fabrics
50cm (22½in) square of brown upholstery fabric for each cushion
A selection of buttons, if desired
Matching thread

Top Tip

For an alternative stripey look, try varying the width of your strips – how about using random strip sizes, or arranging narrow strips working up to wide strips.

Step 4
NEATEN EDGES

Sew a 1/3cm (½in) hem at either end of the rectangle of fabric that is going to be your cushion.

Step 5
SEW CUSHION

With right-sides facing up on a table, fold the left-hand side in and sew along the top and bottom edge. Repeat with the right hand side. The edges should overlap, giving you a pocket that you can put your cushion into when it is turned the right-side out.

STEP 6

Finishing touches

Turn the cushion cover right-sides out and stuff with a cushion pad. Hand sew on buttons, ribbon or your choice of finishing touches.

Flower cushion

Make as above. Cut some simple petal shapes and zigzag stitch in place on the front of your cushion. You could embellish the centre with buttons, felt or a smaller flower shape.

Button cushion

Make as above, but decorate by sewing a selection of small buttons to the front of your cushion, grouped in one corner for a chic effect.

Top Tip
For an alternative stripey look, try varying the width of your strips – how about using random strip sizes, or arranging narrow strips working up to wide strips.

Aromatic Door Stop

Play with layering tiny scraps of fabric and trimmings to make miniature appliqués. Turn them into pretty pendants or practical tags.

About this Pattern

2 ○○○○○ Intermediate

Step 1
CUT TEMPLATE PIECES

Using the dimensions given on the cutting list or your own templates, cut out all the relevant pieces to make your door stop.

Step 2
PREPARE SIDES

Fold the exterior fabric in half width ways with the right sides together and sew down the side. Repeat with the interior fabric side but leave a 6cm (2³⁄₈in) gap for turning.

STEP 3
PREPARE BASE

Pin the exterior circle fabric to the exterior fabric base, right sides together and sew with a 0.5cm (²⁄₈in) seam allowance. Repeat with the interior fabric pieces (Fig. 1).

Step 4
SEW TOGETHER

Place your exterior fabric bag inside the interior fabric bag, right sides together. Pin them in place and then stitch them together around the top (Fig. 2).

FINISHED SIZE
22cm x 15cm (8½in x 6in)

MATERIALS
Patterned exterior fabric
Patterned interior fabric
Plain cotton fabric for the inner bag
Thick garden twine - 2m (79in)
Toy stuffing - 50g
Rice (for filling) - 1.5kg - 2kg
Lavender scented buds - 50g

CUTTING LIST
FROM EXTERIOR FABRIC:
1 x 52cm x 30cm (20½in x 12in)
1 x circle - 15cm (6in) diameter
FROM INTERIOR FABRIC:
1 x 52cm x 30cm (20½in x 12in)
1 x circle - 15cm (6in) diameter
FROM PLAIN COTTON:
1 x 52cm x 30cm (20½in x 12in)
1 x circle - 15cm (6in) diameter

PATTERN NOTES
Seam allowances are 1cm (³⁄₈) unless otherwise stated.

Fig. I

Sew base to side

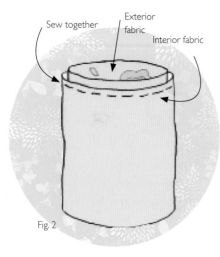

Sew together
Exterior fabric
Interior fabric

Fig. 2

"Make this door stop to any size using any circular template you have handy i.e. a tea plate. Just make sure you adjust the side pieces accordingly."

Turn right-side out by pulling the exterior fabric bag out through the turning gap in the lining. Slip stitch the gap closed by hand and press to iron out any creases and make a neat edge. Top stitch around top edge for reinforcement working with right side uppermost and stitching about 6mm from the fabric edge.

Step 5
MAKE INNER BAG

Neaten one long edge of plain cotton by turning under 2cm (⁶⁄₈in) then tucking raw edge under again. Press and stitch in place close to inner fold. Sew the inner bag together as before and turn right side out. Fill with rice and lavender buds and tie it closed tightly with some twine.

Step 6
COMPLETE DOOR STOP

Place the rice bag inside the fabric bag and stuff the door stop with toy filling to give it more shape. Wind the twine around the top of the door stop as length allows and tie in place with a secure knot or bow (Fig. 3).
Your door stop is now ready to add a delicate fragrance and effortless style to your room.

Fig. 3

Secure twine with knot

Top Tip

You can easily vary the weight of the door stop by using different ratios of rice to stuffing, and by using different types of filling.

Colourful Storage

This storage dumpty is perfect for brightening up and tidying up any room.

About this Pattern

1 ●○○○○ Beginner

FABRIC

Motif fabric: approx 100cm x 100cm (40in x 40in)
Plain fabric for the outer strip: 40cm x 185cm (16in x 72in)

MATERIALS

Zip approx 48cm (19in)

PATTERN NOTES

We used a 1.5cm (⅝in) seam allowance

Step 1

CUT TWO CIRCLES

Cut out two circles, to the size you want your storage dumpty to be. We cut out two large circular motifs from our fabric, each measuring 60cm (23in) in diameter. We formed one of these circles out of two incomplete circles that ran off the edge of the fabric. We joined this circle together with the zip that opens the storage dumpty.

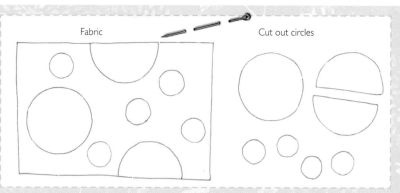

Fabric   Cut out circles

To do this, take one of your two incomplete circles (they need to be larger than semi-circles to allow for seaming) and position the zip along one straight edge, around 2cm (¾in) from the curved edge, right-sides to right-sides. Sew in place on the wrong-side, then fold and iron the seam over to the right-side. Now pin the other incomplete half circle on the other side of the zip, right-sides to right-sides, and check that the pattern on the circles lines up. Sew in place on the wrong-side, then fold and iron the seam over to the right-side.

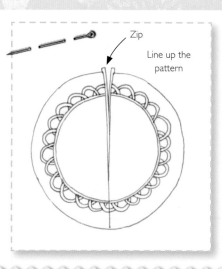

Zip

Line up the pattern

Step 2
CUT THE OUTER STRIP

The finished height of the dumpty will be 37cm (14.5in). Cut the outer strip piece to 40cm (15¾in), to allow for a 1.5cm (½in) seam.

For the circles, at 60cm (23½in) diameter, take off the seam allowance of 1.5cm (½in) on both edges, leaving 57.5cm (225/8in).

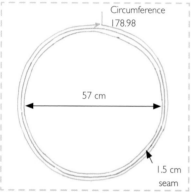

The circumference of a 57cm circle is 179cm (70½in). Add 6cm (2¼in) for the seam allowance, giving a total length for the outer strip of 185cm (73in).

Step 3
DECORATE OUTER STRIP

Next, cut out various shapes and sew them onto your outer strip. You can cut out other sizes of circles from the same fabric and zigzag stitched them onto the strip using red thread. You might wish to pin them or use a temporary adhesive so the shapes stay in place while you sew them on.

Step 4
SEW TOGETHER

Finally, pin the zip circle along one edge of the outer strip, right sides to right sides. Sew together, starting 4cm (1½in) from the end of the outer strip, all the way round

and stopping 4cm (1½in) before the end of the outer strip. Undo the zip and repeat with the other circle on the other side. You should have a small gap not sewn up along the circle edges.

Now pin in place the remaining gap along the circle edges and pin together the end edges of the outer strip.

Remove the pins along the circle edge and sew up the end edges of the outer strip. Iron the seam to one side and re-pin the circle edge and sew up the gap, while also catching down the edges of the side seam.

Step 5
FINISH OFF

To finish, turn the storage dumpty the right-side out and fill with toys, fabric, yarn – whatever you need to tidy up!

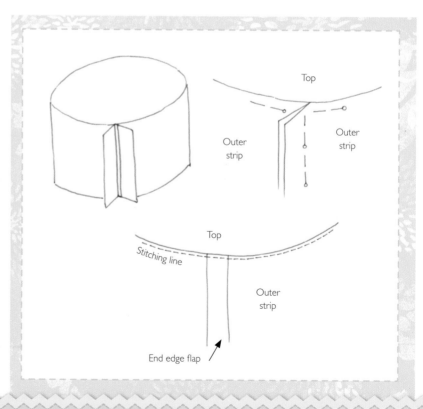

Scrappy Quilt

This pretty quilt is a great way to use up those small pieces of fabric in your stash.

About this Pattern

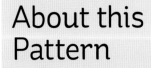

1 ●○○○○ Beginner

Step 1
MAKE BLOCKS

Place a medium square in the top-right corner of a large square and sew into place, approx 0.5cm (²/₈in) from the edge. Place a small square on top, in the top-right corner of the medium square and sew into place approx 0.5cm (²/₈in) from the edge.

Step 2
JOIN BLOCKS

Join four blocks together as shown in the diagram. Repeat these two steps until all your squares have been used.

MATERIALS

18 fat quarters of fabric to make all the blocks for the front of the quilt. You can cut all small squares from two fat quarters or equivalent. You will need 2.25m (87in) of fabric for the back.
Wadding
Thread for quilting

CUTTING LIST

Large squares – cut 36 measuring approx 25cm (10in) square

Medium squares – cut 36 measuring approx 12cm (5in) square

Small squares – cut 36 measuring approx 6cm (2.5in) square

FINISHED SIZE

110cm x 153cm (43in x 60in)

PATTERN NOTES

We used half green, half blue-based fabric for the medium squares and arranged the blocks so the same colours were diagonally opposite each other. The edges of the blocks are intended to be unfinished. You can cut squares using a rotary cutter, or scissors if you don't mind the squares and blocks being slightly different sizes.

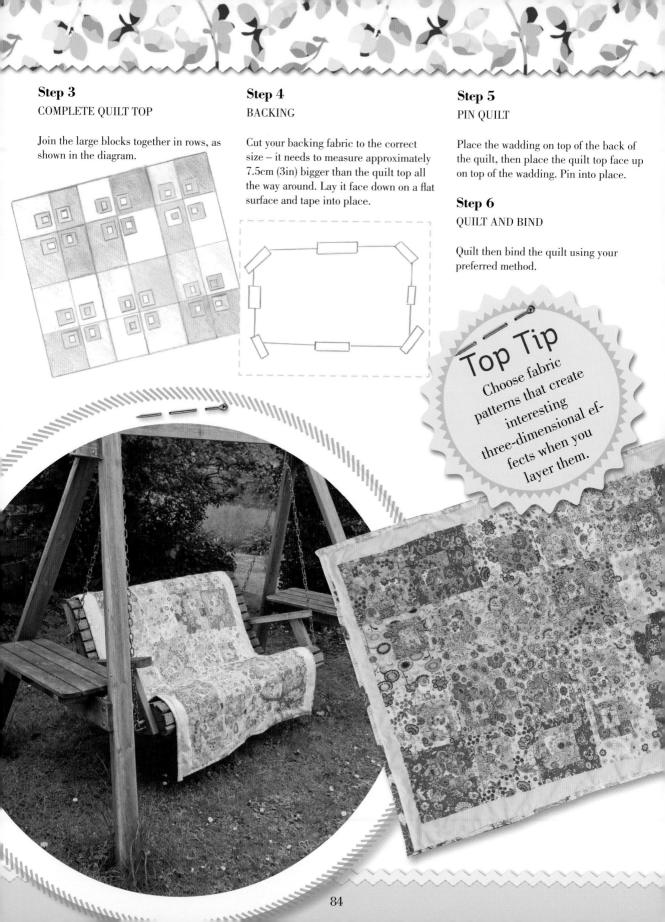

Step 3
COMPLETE QUILT TOP

Join the large blocks together in rows, as shown in the diagram.

Step 4
BACKING

Cut your backing fabric to the correct size – it needs to measure approximately 7.5cm (3in) bigger than the quilt top all the way around. Lay it face down on a flat surface and tape into place.

Step 5
PIN QUILT

Place the wadding on top of the back of the quilt, then place the quilt top face up on top of the wadding. Pin into place.

Step 6
QUILT AND BIND

Quilt then bind the quilt using your preferred method.

Top Tip
Choose fabric patterns that create interesting three-dimensional effects when you layer them.

Scrappy Cushions

A great project for all those little pieces of fabric you might have in your stash.

Step 1
CUT AND JOIN FABRIC SCRAPS

Cut your scraps of fabric into rectangles and squares as per the cutting list. Join the rectangles together three at a time to form a block as shown in the photo (right). Join nine of the squares together to form a block as shown in the photo (right).

Step 2
JOIN BLOCKS INTO STRIPS.

Join four of the blocks of squares together to form one strip. Repeat with the remaining four blocks. Join four of the blocks of rectangles together to form one strip, turning them so that they are a mixture of horizontal and vertical stripes.

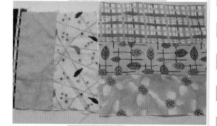

MATERIALS

Cushion front: oddments of fabric.

Cushion back: 1m (1yd) of complementary fabric.

Matching thread

71cm (28in) cushion insert

FINISHED SIZE

Cushion cover is approx 76cm (30in) square, to fit a cushion pad of approx 71cm (28in).

CUTTING LIST

From the scraps of fabric:

24 x rectangles measuring 25cm x 8cm (10in x 3in)

72 x squares measuring 8cm x 8cm (3in x 3in)

From the back fabric:

2 pieces measuring 76cm x 50cm (30in x 20in)

SEAM ALLOWANCE:

1cm (¼in) throughout

PATTERN NOTES

You can also make the back of the cushion from fabric scraps if you have enough, or use two different pieces of fabric for each side.

Step 3

JOIN STRIPS TOGETHER.

Join the four strips together to form a
square shape. Don't worry too much if the
fabrics do not match up entirely or if your
blocks are slightly different shapes.
This will only add to the charm of your
scrappy cushion.

Step 4

JOIN CUSHION FRONT TO BACK

Take the pieces of backing fabrics that
you have cut and hem 1.5cm (½in) around
all four sides. Lay one of the pieces down,
right-sides together, with the patched
cushion front and sew together along
three sides. Repeat with the other backing
piece. The backing pieces will overlap
each other as you are sewing them – this
allows for you to put the cover on the
cushion.

Step 5

FINISH

Turn right
side out.
Press and
insert
cushion pad.

Top Tip

You could use either
all rectangle strips,
or all square strips,
depending on the size
of your scraps.

Tie-dye
Beanbag

A unique addition to any teen's bedroom.
Choose your dyes to coordinate with your décor.

About this Pattern

2 ●●○○○ Intermediate

Step 1
CUT PANEL

Before you start, wash and dry the cotton fabric, then cut a square about 80cm x 80cm (31½in x 31½in).

Step 2
TIE FABRIC

Lay the fabric square on a tabletop. Find the centre of the square (do this by folding into quarters) and pinch the centre between your thumb and forefinger. Start to turn your hand and twist the fabric. It will fold in on itself and form a spiral. Keep twisting until all of the fabric has been drawn into the spiral and you have a bundle roughly circular in shape, if any of the pleats are too high, fold them down. Secure the bundle with elastic bands – you'll need at least three. Make sure all the ends are tucked in so the bundle is tight.

Step 3
PREPARE FABRIC

Put on the plastic gloves, and soak the tied panel for half an hour in a sink full of hot water and soda ash. We recommend filling the sink about half full and using about ¾ cup soda ash. After half an hour, squeeze the excess water out of the bundle (taking care not to upset the arrangement of the folds), and place on a table which you have covered in thick plastic bags.

Step 4
DYE FABRIC

Making sure to wear the gloves, mix your dyes. Put about 2.5 teaspoons of dye in a squeezy bottle, then fill the bottle up about ¾ of the way. Shake and make sure the dye is blended thoroughly. Mix up at least three different colours to make an effective spiral.

Step 5
WASH

The next day, untie your bundle, and unfold it in the sink, rinsing under the tap. When the water is running relatively clear, put the fabric into the washing machine, and wash it with detergent (on its own, or with other tie-dyed stuff) at least 60 degrees. When your fabric has dried, it will be ready to use.

FINISHED SIZE

Circumference - approx 238cm

MATERIALS

Woven cotton (quilting weight) in white or cream - 1m
Bin bags
Soda ash
3 different colours of dye
Rubber bands
Thin plastic gloves
Squeezy bottles with nozzles

PATTERN NOTES

These instructions make a large beanbag – about the same size (perhaps slightly bigger) as a standard bag. You can very easily adjust the measurements to make a smaller or larger one, or a cushion.

The quantities of dye given below normally dye about 4-5 items. Since you have to get out all your bin bags and rubber gloves anyway, why not do a t-shirt or old pillowcase at the same time? Of course, you can also halve the dye quantities.

MAKE PATTERN: To make the spiral pattern – Make a triangle with the point in the middle of the spiral. Repeat with the other colours and alternate triangle sections. Repeat on the back of the bundle. The dyes will run into each other so don't worry. Squirt the dye into the folds of the fabric – this will give a greater colour intensity on your finished panel. Now leave the dyed bundle overnight.

Sew Beanbag

A colourful addition to any teen's bedroom.

About this Pattern

1 ●○○○○ Beginner

Step 1
CUT FABRIC

Out of the square tie-dyed fabric, cut a circle that is 76cm (30in) across. The easiest way to do this is to put a pin in the centre of the square (this will be obvious as it's a spiral), and measure 38cm (16in) all round at points about 7cm (2¾in) apart, marking with chalk. This will be enough for you to draw a circle. When you have cut out your circle, fold it into quarters to check that the top edge is even. Trim as necessary.

Step 2
CUT BEANBAG BOTTOM

Fold this circle in half and use it as a template to cut out the bottom of the beanbag from the 1m (1yd) of fabric.

Step 3
PIECE TOGETHER

For a 76cm (30in) circle, you will need to make a strip 238cm (93¾in) long plus a 1cm (⅛in) seam allowance. Aim to make a strip about 245cm (96½in), which will give you room for error. Choose a selection of fabrics which tone with the colours in the dyed panel (or contrast with it). Cut strips of different widths, all 35cm (13¾in) long. This will make your beanbag about 32cm (13in) high – if you would like it either flatter or taller just adjust the length of your strip. Allow a 1cm (⅜in) seam on your pieces. Sew your strip together and press the seams open.

STEP 4
ATTACH SIDE PANEL

Pin the right side of the strip to the right side of the top panel, being careful to keep the circle shape intact. Use this to judge how long your pieced strip needs to be (remembering the seam allowance) – sew the ends of the pieced strip so it forms a circle (being careful not to twist it). You should be able to do this without unpinning all the top panel, just the bit where the seam is. Sew the top panel to the pieced strip using a 1cm (⅜in) seam allowance. Press the seam towards the pieced strip.

Step 5
SEW TO BOTTOM

Pin and sew the strip to the bottom piece,

MATERIALS

Dyed fabric - 80cm x 80cm (31½in x 31½in)
Cotton fabric - 1m (1yd)
Assortment of scraps, 35cm (13¾in) long, enough to make a strip about 245cm (96½in) long when sewn together
Bags of beanbag beads for stuffing

PATTERN NOTES

These instructions are for a beanbag which is stuffed and then sewn closed, as this is the easiest and quickest way to do it: it will mean, however, that you can't remove the cover to wash it (or, not without removing all the stuffing first). If you prefer, you can make a removable cover by following the instructions below to make an inner cushion, then sew the outer bag in exactly the same way (same measurements) but insert a zip into the bottom seam.

leaving a 26cm (10¼in) gap for stuffing. Turn the beanbag to the right side.

Step 6
STUFF

Stuff with the beanbag filling (it's easiest to use a jug and accept that you're going to have to hoover afterwards). The filling will settle a little in use so stuff quite full, but don't overstuff. Sew the gap closed and your beanbag is ready.

Top Tip

You can mix colours of Procion dyes – feel free to experiment – but if this is your first attempt it might be easier to use them as they come.

Simple Apron

Made from just two tea towels, this apron is stylish and simple to make.

About this Pattern

1 ○○○○○ **Beginner**

Step 1
SEW TEA TOWELS TOGETHER

Take both tea towels and lay them together right sides facing out. Sew around three of the edges approx 1cm (¼in) from the edge, just inside the seam of the tea towels.

Step 2
PREPARE STRAPS

Cut two pieces of fabric measuring 65cm (25in) by 1cm (2in). Fold in half, neaten edge and sew along long side.

Step 3
ATTACH STRAPS

Sew the straps, one either side, of the top of the apron.

MATERIALS
- White sewing thread
- 2 x tea towels
- Either a third tea towel for ties or piece of material measuring 10cm (4in) by 65cm (25in)

Simple Throw

Made from just two tea towels, this apron
is stylish and simple to make.

About this Pattern

1 ⬤◯◯◯◯ Beginner

Step 1
TRIM FLEECE

Cut your fleece blanket to the exact size
given in the materials list.

Step 2
CUT COTTON FABRIC

Cut your cotton fabric into 4 strips measuring 5cm (2in) longer than the length of
your fleece blanket by 24cm (10in).

Step 3
PRESS COTTON FABRIC

Fold the strips of cotton fabric in half so
that they measure 12cm (5in) by 5cm (2in)
longer than he length of your fleece blanket. Press. Unfold the strips and turn the
raw long edges 2cm (³/₄in) to the inside.
Press each turn. Repeat with all 4 strips.

Step 4
ATTACH COTTON STRIPS

Take the first cotton strip and pin into
place along one of the sides of your fleece
blanket. Ensure that the pressed edge
in the middle of the strip is comfortably
against the edge of the blanket. Hand sew
into place on
both sides. Repeat for opposite side
of blanket.

Step 5
PREPARE FINAL STRIPS

Take the 2 final strips and turn the short
edges in by 2.5cm (1in) each end.
Press to form a neat edge.

Step 6
ATTACH FINAL STRIPS

Sew the final 2 strips to the fleece blanket
ensuring that the edges are neat.

MATERIALS

Fleece blanket measuring
140cm x 100cm (55in x 40in)

1.5m (1.75yd) cotton fabric

Matching thread

Sewing needle

Pins

Scrappy Napkin

Use up those small pieces of fabric you have leftover to make these almost matching napkins – perfect for dinner parties or picnics!

About this Pattern

1 ○○○○ Beginner

MATERIALS

Scraps of fabric measuring a total of approx 30cm x 20cm (12in x 8in) for each side of each napkin

Pinking sheers

Contrasting thread

FINISHED SIZE

Each napkin measures approx 30cm x 20cm (12in x 8in). If you make them slightly different sizes, you'll have a more eclectic collection!

Step 1
CHOOSE YOUR FABRICS

Choose the fabrics that you are going to use for your first napkin and join the scraps together to measure approx 30cm x 20cm (12in x 8in). Repeat to prepare a second side for your napkin using other scraps.

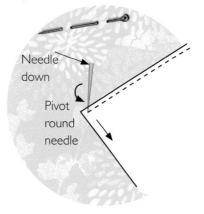

Needle down

Pivot round needle

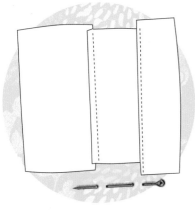

Step 2
JOIN TOGETHER

With wrong-sides together, sew around your two pieces of fabric, approx 1.5cm (⅝in) from the edge, using a contrasting thread. When it comes to the corners, move your needle to the down position and turn the napkin so that you can sew neatly without any movement of the stitches.

Step 3
EDGING

Using pinking sheers, cut close to the line of contrast stitching, leaving approx 0.5cm (¼in) between the stitching and the edge of the napkins. This gives a decorative finish to your napkin.

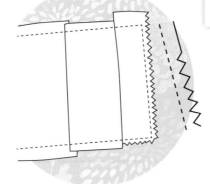

Step 4
OPTIONAL EXTRAS

These napkins are a great way to experiment with new fabric collections or to use up scraps of fabric. They can be embellished using buttons, ribbon, ric-rac or anything else you have available to personalise your napkins.

Pocket Banner

This rose-shaped pocket banner will brighten and adorn any room, perfect for parties and summer events.

About this Pattern

2 ●●○○○ Intermediate

Part 1: Make the banner

Step 1
PLAN YOUR BANNER

Decide how long you wish to make your banner. Leave a gap of 10cm (4in) between each pocket on the banner, plus 26cm (10in) of tape at each end. You can change any of these measurements to suit you.

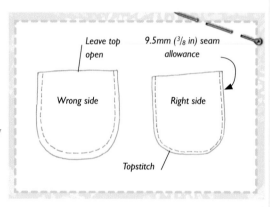

Leave top open

9.5mm (³/₈ in) seam allowance

Wrong side

Right side

Topstitch

Step 2
MAKE POCKET PANELS

Cut two of pocket shapes measuring approx 18cm tall and 12cm wide for each panel of the banner. Cut one pocket shape in the lightweight interfacing and fuse onto one of the pocket panels. With right sides together, stitch the front and back pocket panels together around the curved edge, leaving the top open. Turn right side out and press. On the right side, topstitch a neat line around the curved edge of the pocket, around ½in from the edge.

Part 2: Make appliqué flowers

Step 1
CUT PETALS

To create the appliqué posie panel, cut 5 of Petal 1 (large petal shape measuring approx 8cm tall by 4cm wide), 3 of Petal 2 (measuring approx 5cm tall by 3cm wide) and 2 of Petal 3 (measuring approx 4cm tall by 2.5cm wide) . Arrange these on your panel. If you like, use some temporary adhesive to hold your petals in place while you sew them on.

MATERIALS

Double-sided bias tape, the length of your banner

Fat quarters of various different fabrics

Large buttons

Stuffing

Lightweight interfacing

Tailor's chalk

PATTERN NOTES

The seam allowance is 1.5cm (½in) unless otherwise noted.

The banner can be adjusted to suit your fancy! Make each panel the 3D version of the flower or make each panel with the simple appliqué. Or mix it up, as shown here. You can leave this banner up all year round to decorate a child's room, so try to mix up the seasonal feel of the fabrics used.

Step 2
SEW PETALS

Sew around each petal at least twice and don't be neat. Stitch a button in the centre to finish.

Note: This stitching will be visible at the back of each pocket panel, so beware if the banner will be seen from the reverse side. Alternatively, decorate the front of your pocket panel before sewing it to the back.

Step 3
FINISH OFF

Now find a wonderful big button for the centre and stitch in place. Repeat the process above for each appliqué posie panel you wish to make.

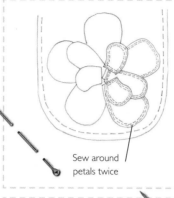

Sew around petals twice

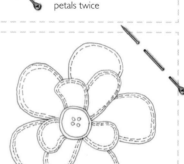

Part 3: Make 3D flowers

Step 1
CUT PETALS

For each 3D version of the posies panel, you will need to cut 10 of Petal 1, 10 of Petal 2 and 6 of Petal 3. Petal 1 is the outer tier of your posie, Petal 2 is your second tier, and Petals 3 your inner or first tier.

Step 2
STUFFED PETALS

Place two Petal 1 shapes together, wrong sides facing. Stitch around the curved edge ½in from the edge, leaving the bottom of the petal open. Stuff each petal lightly, just enough to give it some structure. You will have raw edges that will fray, but that's part of the charm of this banner. Repeat this

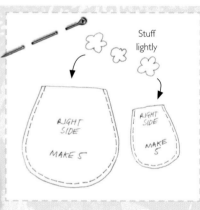

Stuff lightly

RIGHT SIDE
MAKE 5

RIGHT SIDE
MAKE 5

with all other Petal 1 and Petal 2 shapes.

Step 3
INNER PETALS

Now place two Petal 3 shapes together, wrong sides facing. Stitch around the curved edge ½in from the edge and also add a stitched circular pattern or any stitch you choose to decorate the petal. Leave the bottom of the petal open, although these inner tier petals will not be

stuffed. Repeat with the rest of the Petal 3 shapes.

Step 4
MARK THE CENTRE

Take one of your pocket panels and fold in half, then in half again to find the centre of your panel. Using your chalk, trace around a thread spool to give you a centre on which to focus as you pin your flower petals onto the panel.

Step 5
STITCH OUTER TIER

Arrange all of your layers first to determine how they will lay on your panel. Once you get them to your liking, pin tier 3 and remove the rest. Stitch the tier 3 petals to the pocket panel in a circle, lightly gathering or pinching each petal a little to pull the edges closer to the circle and also close each petal opening.

Step 6
STITCH SECOND TIER

Layer your tier 2 petals on top of tier 3 and again, sew a small central circle to secure

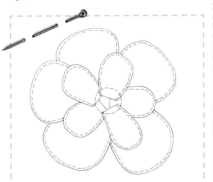

each petal and close the opening at the end.

Step 7
STITCH CENTRAL TIER

Finally, layer your tier 1 petals on top of tier 2 and sew a small central circle to secure each petal and close the opening at the end.

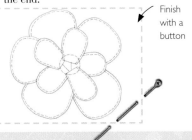

Finish with a button

Note: This stitching will be visible at the back of each pocket panel, so beware if the banner will be seen from the reverse side. Alternatively, decorate the front of your pocket panel before sewing it to the back.

Step 8
FINISH OFF

Now find a wonderful big button for the centre and stitch in place. Repeat the process above for each 3D posy panel you wish to make.

Part 4: Finish the banner

Once you have all of your flower panels constructed, cut your double-sided bias tape to the length you want your banner to be. Now lay out your panels spaced evenly onto the bias tape. Tuck each panel inside the bias tape and pin to secure. Stitch all the way down the length of the bias tape to attach all the panels. Hang and enjoy!

Stitch down

Patchwork Table Runner

Table runners can be beautifully quilted or embellished. This one uses scraps of fabric to create a stylish look for your kitchen table.

About this Pattern

1 ●○○○○ Beginner

Step 1
CHOOSE YOUR FABRICS

Choose the fabrics that you are going to use for your table runner and join your scraps together in a long length, which measures 30cm x 144cm (12in x 57in). Prepare a second side for your table runner using other scraps. We used pieces of fabric that were all 30cm (12in) wide but were different lengths – if you chose to use smaller pieces of fabric, your table runner would have a more patchwork feel to it.

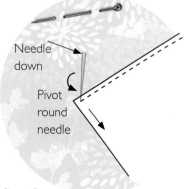

Needle down

Pivot round needle

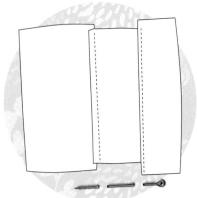

Step 2
JOIN TOGETHER

With wrong sides together, sew around your two pieces of fabric, approx 1.5cm (¹/₈in) from the edge, using contrasting thread. When it comes to the corners, move your needle to the down position and turn the table runner so that you can sew neatly without any movement of the stitches.

Step 3
EDGING

Using the pinking shears, cut close to the line of contrast stitching, leaving approx 0.5cm (²/₈in) between the stitching and the edge of the table runner. This gives a decorative finish.

MATERIALS

Scraps of fabric measuring a total of approx 30cm x 150cm (12in x 20in) for each side of your table runner

Pinking sheers

Contrasting thread

FINISHES

30cm x 144cm (12in x 59in)

Step 4
OPTIONAL EXTRAS

Your table runner is now ready to be embellished using buttons, ribbon, ric-rac or anything else that you want to sew on to personalise it. You could sew ribbon at most of the fabric changes, to highlight the movement of the fabrics, or add beads or buttons to the edge of your runner, or use two very different colourways on either side of the runner for two looks in one!

Horse Lavendar
Sachets

Make these delightfully sweet smelling lavender
horses to hang in your wardrobe. Of course,
any other shape or animal will also work.

About this Pattern

2 ●○○○○ Intermediate

FINISHED SIZE

Each horse: approx 10cm (4in)

MATERIALS

15cm (6in) square printed cotton

15cm (6in) square backing fabric
to match

20cm (8in) ribbon for hanging loop

Polyester fibre filling

Small amount of dried lavender

A selection of buttons

Suitable stuffing tool

PATTERN NOTES

All seam allowances are 1cm (½cm)

This pattern uses shapes and images that are already printed on your
chosen fabric. The finished articles
can be any shape or size, just make
sure you have enough backing fabric
to match.

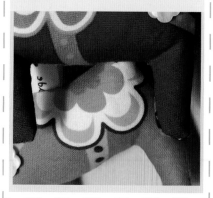

Step 1

PREPARE SHAPES

Select the horse or other shape on the
cloth you want to use and cut out a square
around it. Cut a matching square of
backing fabric. Cut your ribbon to the
required length.

Step 2

ATTACH RIBBON

Fold the length of ribbon in half and pin
it to the right-side top edge of one horse
section. Make sure the raw edges are lined
up, then pin the backing fabric over the
top, right sides together, sandwiching the
ribbon. Take care to roll up the loop end of
the ribbon so that it doesn't get caught up
in the stitching (Fig. 1).

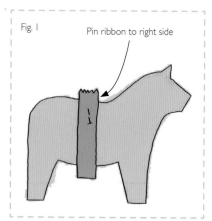

Fig. I   Pin ribbon to right side

Step 3

PIN IN PLACE

It is usually quite easy to pin across the
outline of the horse shape and to sew
around it, but if the shape looks faint or
you feel unsure, trace the outline through
onto the wrong side of the fabric first with
some tailor's chalk.

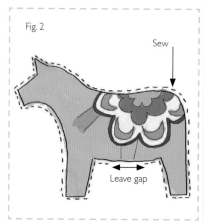

Fig. 2   Sew   Leave gap

Step 4

SEW TOGETHER

Taking your time, machine stitch carefully
around the outline of the horse, leaving
a gap big enough for turning and stuffing
along the belly. The size of this gap will be
dependant on the size of the shape you
are using (Fig. 2).

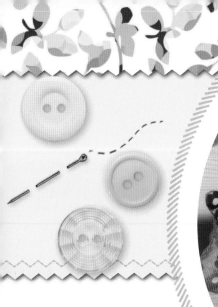

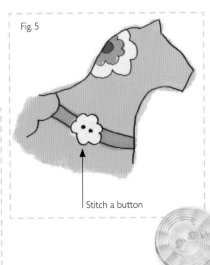

Step 5
TRIM AND TURN

Remove the pins and trim the seams, making sure not to cut too close to the stitching. Turn right-side out and press (fig 3).

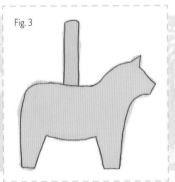

Fig. 3

Step 7
FINISH

Hand stitch the gap closed using a ladder stitch and finish by embellishing your horse with a button (fig 5).

Top Tip
To provide a dirt resist finish, spray the fabric parts of the bag with stain resistant spray.

Step 6
STUFF

Generously stuff the horse with a mix of lavender and polyester filling. Doing this inside a clear plastic bag saves a lot of mess (fig 4).

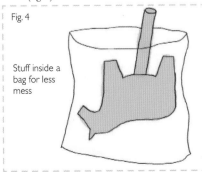

Fig. 4

Stuff inside a bag for less mess

Fig. 5

Stitch a button

Three mix-and-match scented horses make a lovely present if you're on a budget. Who wouldn't want an aromatic wardrobe?

Children's

What could be more satisfying to sew than a quilt for a newborn baby's cot? With this section full of fun, playful projects, you can create something truly special for a tiny tot.

Baby Sling

This simple sling is the perfect project for expecting mums, but also makes a lovely maternity gift.

About this Pattern

1 ○○○○○ Beginner

Step 1

DETERMINE SIZE OF SLING

Measure the person that the sling is going to be for, from one shoulder to the opposite hip, then multiply that measurement by three – a total length of 2.3m (2½ yard) is enough for most people, although it's better to make the sling slightly too big than too small.

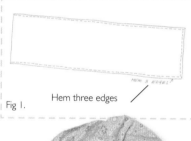

Fig 1. — Hem three edges

Step 2

PREPARE YOUR FABRIC

Cut your fabric to 92cm (36in) wide along the length. Hem both of the long edges and one of the short edges (fig. 1).

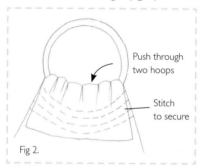

Push through two hoops

Stitch to secure

Fig 2.

Step 3

ATTACH THE RINGS

Lay both rings on top of each other. Take the short edge of the fabric that you did not seam and pull it through the rings so that approx. 13-15cm (5-6in) is pulled through. Pin in place and sew all the way across the fabric from one side to the other. This sewing needs to be very secure, so use a small stitch and try to make sure you have plenty of rows sewn – we zig-zagged all
the way up, keeping the lines approx 0.5cm (¼in) apart.

Step 4

FINISHING OFF

Gather the tail of the sling and thread it through both rings, then back over one and under the other one. You're ready to go!

SIZE

One size should fit all

MATERIALS

2.3m (2.5 yds) of cotton fabric

Matching thread

2 sling rings

HOW TO WEAR YOUR SLING

First decide on which shoulder you would like your sling to rest. Starting from the opposite side, put your arm through the sling and lift it over your head. Adjust the sling so that the rings sit just in front of your shoulder. Reaching behind you, spread the sling material out across your back and on top of your shoulder. Finally, open out the sling at the front, making the pouch where the baby will sit. Once worn, the sling can be used to carry a baby in various ways. It can be used to seat a baby vertically (facing forwards or backwards) or carry them straddling your hip.

Cosy Quilt

Make your newborn as snug as a bug in a rug with this exquisite eiderdown quilt.

Step 1

PREPARE SANDWICH

Place one piece of fabric, right-side up, on a flat surface. Place the second piece of fabric on top of it, right-side down, so that the two right sides are facing each other. Place the wadding on top of them.

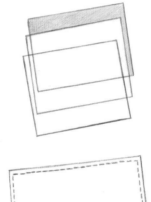

Step 2

SEW EDGES

Sew all around the edge of the quilt, leaving a 6in gap to turn it the right-side out.

Step 3

SEW GAP CLOSED

Sew the gap closed using a neat, invisible stitch.

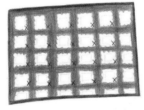

Step 4

TIE

If you choose to, you can either use a quilting foot and machine stitch a grid pattern over the quilt, or use the embroidery thread and sew small cross stitches to fuse the quilt at regular intervals.

MATERIALS

1.8m square (2 square yds) of cotton fabric (we used two different fabrics – one for the front and one for the back).

1.8m square (1 square yard) of wadding. This needs to be approx the same size as your front and back fabrics.

Matching thread

Embroidery thread for ties

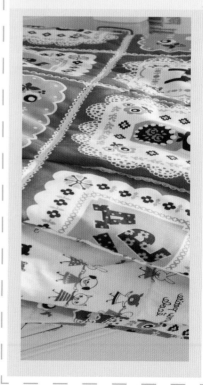

Top Tip
You can use whole pieces of fabric or join smaller pieces together to make up the size that you need.

Drawstring
Skirt

Make your little one as pretty as a picture
in this simple-to-make skirt!

About this Pattern

1 ⬤○○○○ **Beginner**

Step 1

CUT FABRIC

Cut a piece of fabric as per the cutting list.

Step 2

HEM AND CREATE CHANNEL FOR ELASTIC

With the wrong-side facing up, turn
a 2cm (¾in) hem at the bottom of the
fabric and sew into place. Turn the
top of the fabric down 1cm (⅜in),
press and then turn down a further 3cm
(1⅛in) to create a channel for the elastic
to be inserted. Press and then sew
into place.

Step 3

TRIM BOTTOM EDGE

If you wish, this is the time to sew on your
decorative trim at the bottom of the skirt.
With the right-side facing up, pin your
ribbon, ricrac or chosen embellishment
to the bottom of your skirt and sew into
place.

Step 4

SEW SIDE SEAMS

Zig-zag stitch the raw edges of the skirt
and then, with right-sides facing, sew
side seams, ensuring that you sew
through only one layer of the fabric at
the top where the elastic channel is.

Step 5

INSERT ELASTIC

Insert your elastic through the waistband
channel and secure. Sew the gap closed
and wear!

Top Tip

You can use any fabric for
this skirt – we found that
dressmaking or quilting weight
cotton worked best, but
upholstery weight will still
work, albeit resulting in a
heavier weight
skirt.

MATERIALS

1m (1 yd) of fabric
1m (1 yd) of elastic for waistband
1–2m (1–2 yd) of contrast ribbon,
ricrac or other embellishment for
bottom of skirt (optional)

FINISHED SIZE

2–3 years – 30cm (12in) long
4–5 years – 35cm (14in) long
6–7 years – 40cm (16in) long
8–9 years – 45cm (18in) long
10–11 years – 50cm (20in) long

CUTTING LIST

Age – width x length
2–3 years – 1m (1 yd) x 38cm (15in)
4–5 years – 1m (1 yd) x 43cm (17in)
6–7 years – 1m (1 yd) x 48cm (19in)
8–9 years – 1m (1 yd) x 53cm (21in)
10–11 years – 1m (1 yd) x 58cm (23in)

T-shirt
Hat & Scarf

Repurpose an old, long-sleeved jersey T-shirt into this quick and easy kid's hat-and-scarf set.

About this Pattern

1 ○○○○○ **Beginner**

MATERIALS

An adult-sized, long-sleeved T-shirt
Matching thread

Step 1

HAT

This hat is to fit a child aged 4 - 8. Draw a hat template using the shape below as a guide. The hat needs to be 23cm (9in) wide and approx 20cm (8in) tall with rounded edges as shown. Lay your T-shirt down on a flat surface and place your template along the bottom edge. Doing this ensures that you don't have to seam the bottom of the hat. Pin template into place and cut through both layers of the T-shirt, giving you two pieces of hat.

Join together around the curved edge, with right-sides facing, using a 1cm (³/₈ in) seam allowance. Turn right-way round and neaten seams.

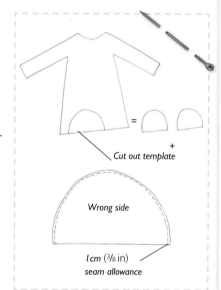

Cut out template

Wrong side

1cm (³/₈ in) seam allowance

Step 2

SCARF

We used both sleeves and a section from the front of the T-shirt to make this scarf. Cut pieces of fabric from the leftovers of your T-shirt to make a scarf that measures 1m (1 yd) long. Join the pieces together and allow the edges of the jersey to roll inwards – they will not require any finishing.

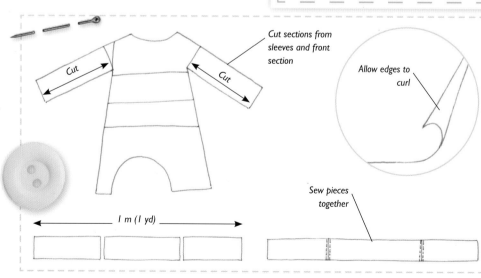

Cut

Cut

Cut sections from sleeves and front section

Allow edges to curl

Sew pieces together

1 m (1 yd)

Top Tip

Try a printed or patterned top for a little more interest in your hat and scarf set. Or use your child's favourite old T-shirt to make a super-special hat!

Pillowcase
Dresses

These dresses were made from odd pillowcases.
They're great to use as painting overalls.

About this Pattern

1 ○○○○○ Beginner

Step 1
PREPARATION

Wash and iron your pillowcase.

Step 2
CUT FOR LENGTH

Measure the distance from the child's
shoulder blade to where you want the
dress to fall to and add 2.5cm (1in).

Mark this on the pillowcase and cut off
the closed edge at the point you have
marked.

Step 3
MAKE ARMHOLES

Fold the pillowcase in half widthwise
and mark out the armholes as shown in
the sketch below. The piece you cut out
should be 5cm wide and 15cm deep. Cut
out the arm holes.

SIZE

One pillow case will make a dress to
fit a child up to the age of 10.

MATERIALS
• 1 pillow case
• Approx 1m (1 yd) of ribbon

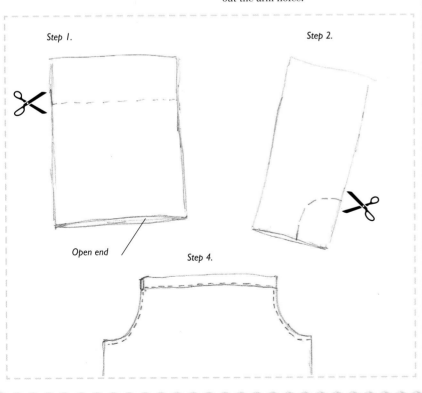

Step 1.

Open end

Step 2.

Step 4.

Top Tip

For winter dresses we used flannelette pillow cases. Use cotton ones for more dresses to be worn in spring and summer.

White version made from flannel pillowcase and embellished with buttons. Pink version made from flannel pillowcase and armholes bound with the same Cath Kidston fabric that was used for the ribbon tie. The bright patterned version made from a handmade Amy Butler pillowcase bought from a flea market.

Step 4
SEAM ARMHOLES

Turn inside out and press a 1.5cm (½in) seam around the armholes to the wrong side. Stitch into place.

Step 5
CHANNEL FOR RIBBON

Fold over 2.5cm (1in) at the top of the front of the pillowcase to form a casing for the ribbon to go through. Stitch into place. Repeat for the back.

Step 6
ADD TIES

Cut the ribbon in half. Thread one piece through the front and one piece through the back channel. Pull and gather, then tie at the top of the shoulders to keep the

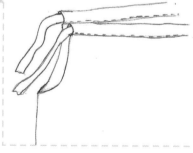

Step 5.

dress on. Alternatively, if you prefer, move the ribbons through the channel so that the tied sections are not showing.

Step 7
EMBELLISH

The hem at the bottom of the pillowcase makes the hem at the bottom of your dress. If you prefer, you can hem along the 'envelope' part of the case and cut out the excess fabric. Decorate with, ribbon or other finishing as desired.

Embellishment by
Appliqué

Give a T-shirt new life with appliqué stitching.

About this Pattern

1 ⬤◯◯◯◯ Beginner

Step 1
FIND APPLIQUÉ DESIGN

Draw or copy a design suitable for appliqué. Children's colouring books are a good source as the illustrations have simple outlines or create a flower with circles, ovals and leaf shapes. Divide the design into parts of different colours.

Step 2
IRON FUSIBLE WEBBING

Cut rectangles of fusible webbing large enough for each part of the design and iron these to the wrong side of the coloured fabrics. On the paper, draw the outline of each shape. If the design is not symmetrical remember to draw the shape in reverse so that it will appear the correct way when stuck down.

Step 3
CUT SHAPES

Cut out each part of the shape and peel off the backing paper. Arrange these in position, a little like a jigsaw, then iron carefully to fuse them in place (fig 1).

Sew in place with either a contrast thread or one that matches depending on the effect required (contrasting thread will form a bold outline and make the design more prominent). Use a zigzag stitch with a reduced length to produce a satin stitch that gives a bolder line. The approximate setting of the stitch will be 3mm wide and 0.3mm long. This may be marked in stitches per inch on other machines in which case the setting should be approximately eight stitches per inch wide and 20 stitches per inch long. Try the stitch on an off-cut

FINISHED SIZE

This will vary according to your design and the item you are embellishing.

MATERIALS

Plain T-shirt

Brightly colored plain or printed fabric scraps to use for the appliqué designs

One pack of fusible webbing
Contrasting or matching sewing thread as desired

Tear-away stabiliser

of fabric and adjust to achieve a solid band of stitching before starting to sew on the design.

Step 4
ADD STITCHING

Complete the design with any other lines and stitches over the appliqué or round the collar, cuffs or hem of the T-shirt. Many modern sewing machines have a wide range of decorative stitches to choose from but a range of simple straight and zigzag stitches can look just as effective, too.a

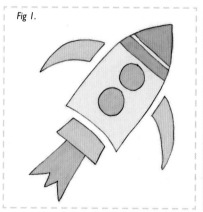

Fig 1.

Top Tip

When sewing directly onto the T-shirt fabric use a tear away stabiliser undearneath the stabiliser tears away completely aftewards.

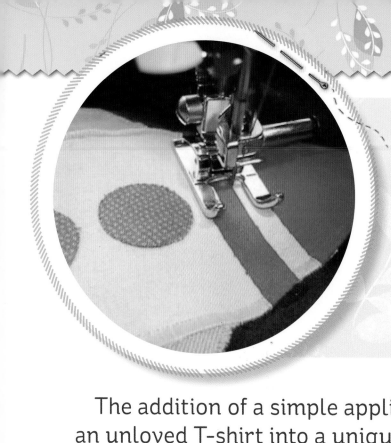

No sewing machine?

If you do not have a sewing machine it is easy to sew the appliqué in place with blanket stitches sewn by hand. Use an embroidery thread (either three strands of stranded embroidery thread or pearle cotton) in a contrasting colour and form the stitches around the outside of the design.

The addition of a simple appliqué motif can make an unloved T-shirt into a uniquely designed creation. Recycling or up-cycling clothing has been a popular theme in recent years. It allows a 'new' garment to be created with little or no cost to you or to the environment.

Applique know-how

● Appliqué is a technique where, as the name implies, a piece of fabric is applied to the surface of another. The method produces a bold embellishment that is easy to create compared with the more time-consuming skill of embroidery. It has the added benefit of being 'green' as it can use up unwanted fabrics; off-cuts from other projects or unwanted, out-dated or worn-out clothing. All are perfect for producing appliqué designs.

● Bondaweb is a heat-fusible glue layer on a paper base. The glue is in the form of a film backed with the paper (to make handling easier), which melts and fuses when heated. Iron it to the back of a fabric, cut out a shape, peel off the backing paper and place it where required on a garment then iron it in position. This does away with the need to tack or baste the shape in place by hand before sewing it securely in position.

● Stabiliser is a bonded layer of material used under the fabric during stitching to support the stitches and allow a better finish to be produced. The most common variety is the tearaway stabiliser that is torn off after stitching. Other varieties of this include soluble (washaway) and heataway stabilisers.

● Satin stitch is a machine zigzag stitch which has been shortened to give a bold line.

Simple Children's
Clothes

Sometimes the very best revamps are the most simple.

About this Pattern

1 ○○○○○ Beginner

MATERIALS
A T-shirt that fits your child
0.5m (½ yd) of lightweight fabric (voile or quilters cotton works well)
Matching thread
Needle

TIME TAKEN
An hour

Lay the T-shirt down on a flat surface and measure all around the bottom, recording the measurement on a piece of paper.

The fabric for the skirt needs to measure approximately 25cm (10in) deep by two times the circumference of your T-shirt. Cut to size.

Fold the bottom of the fabric up 1cm (³⁄₈in) and press. Fold up again and hand stitch hem in place. Press the side seams in by 1cm (³⁄₈in) and then repeat. With right-sides facing, stitch the side seam together.

Sew two rows of large stitches around the top of the skirt to use as gathering stitches. Do not secure the end.

With the T-shirt the correct way up on the table, place the skirt piece inside out and around the T-shirt so that the neat hem is at the top and the gathered edge is at the bottom of the T-shirt.

The T-shirt should fit neatly inside the skirt. Pull the gathering strings until the skirt is the same size as the T-shirt.

Pin and then sew in place with the gathered edge of the skirt fitting inside the T-shirt.

Loopy-Ribbon
Soother

Babies will love the different colours and textures of this simple ribbon-edged soother.

About this Pattern

1 ●○○○○ Beginner

Step 1
SELECTING RIBBONS

To make this soother you will need to cut 16 strips of ribbon, each measuring 8cm (3in). Experiment with colours and patterns, the more variety the better! We have used a selection in bright primary colours with bold patternas and varying widths and textures.

Step 2
SIZING UP

Next, cut two squares of cotton fabric, each measuring 22cm (8⅝in). We have used cotton seersucker and woven pin-stripe cotton in pale greens. To get two really precise edges with perfect square corners quilting ruler to cut the fabric. If you don't have them, scissors and a tape measure can be just as good.

> "This project is perfect for using up small scraps of fabric and ribbon scraps in your stash."

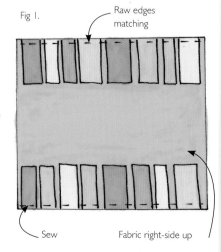

Fig 1.

Raw edges matching

Sew

Fabric right-side up

Step 3
START TO STITCH

Fold your ribbon pieces in half. With the right side of your fabric facing up, sew eight of your ribbon pieces to one side of the fabric with the raw edges matching around 3mm (⅛in) from the edge. Reverse the machine several times over each ribbon to make sure it's really secure. Repeat on the opposite edge of your fabric (fig 1).

Step 4
SEW TOGETHER

Place the two fabric squares together, with right-sides facing and the ribbons sandwiched in-between. Sew around the edge using a 6mm (¼in) seam leaving a 8cm (3in) gap between the start and end of your sewing to turn your soother inside out.

FINISHED SIZE

20cm x 20cm (7⅞in x 7⅞in)

MATERIALS

Cotton fabric – 22cm x 50cm (8⅝in x 19⅝in)
16 different ribon scraps – each 8cm (3in) long

CUTTING LIST

From cotton fabric:

2 x squares – 22cm x 22cm (8⅝in x 8⅝in)

PATTERN NOTES

The seam allowance for this pattern is 6mm (¼in)

Step 5
FINISHING TOUCHES

Turn your soother inside out and press with a warm iron. Finally, overstitch the gap in the seam and your soother is now finished!

Top Tip

This project is perfect for using up small scraps of fabric and ribbon in your stash.

Hair Clip
Flower

A simple but beautiful daisy clip, perfect for any summer outfit.

About this Pattern

1 ●○○○○ **Beginner**

MATERIALS

Plain hair clip

Scraps of white fabric

Scraps of yellow felt

Matching thread

Needle

TIME TAKEN

An hour

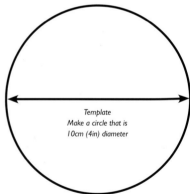

Template
Make a circle that is
10cm (4in) diameter

Transfer the circle template below onto some card or paper. Using the template, draw around and cut out five circles of white fabric. Scallop the edges of three of the circles using scissors to resemble petals.

Place the circles on top of each other with the shaped ones on the top. Cut a small circle of yellow felt and sew in the centre of the five white circles, fixing them together with the needle and thread sew on a hair clip.